ROUTLEDGE LIBRARY EDITIONS:
WELFARE AND THE STATE

Volume 13

THE STRATEGY OF
EQUALITY

THE STRATEGY OF EQUALITY
Redistribution and the Social Services

JULIAN LE GRAND

Routledge
Taylor & Francis Group

LONDON AND NEW YORK

First published in 1982 by George Allen and Unwin (Publishers) Ltd

This edition first published in 2019

by Routledge

2 Park Square, Milton Park, Abingdon, Oxon OX14 4RN

and by Routledge

711 Third Avenue, New York, NY 10017

Routledge is an imprint of the Taylor & Francis Group, an informa business

© 1982 Julian Le Grand

British Library Cataloguing in Publication Data
A catalogue record for this book is available from the British Library

ISBN: 978-1-138-61373-7 (Set)
ISBN: 978-0-429-45813-2 (Set) (ebk)
ISBN: 978-1-138-59744-0 (Volume 13) (hbk)
ISBN: 978-1-138-59765-5 (Volume 13) (pbk)
ISBN: 978-0-429-48685-2 (Volume 13) (ebk)

Publisher's Note

The publisher has gone to great lengths to ensure the quality of this reprint but points out that some imperfections in the original copies may be apparent.

Disclaimer

The publisher has made every effort to trace copyright holders and would welcome correspondence from those they have been unable to trace.

The Strategy of Equality

Redistribution and the Social Services

JULIAN LE GRAND

Lecturer in Economics, London School of Economics

London
GEORGE ALLEN & UNWIN

Boston   Sydney

**George Allen & Unwin (Publishers) Ltd,
40, Museum Street, London, WC1A 1LU, UK**

George Allen & Unwin (Publishers) Ltd,
Park Lane, Hemel Hempstead, Herts, HP2 4TE, UK

Allen & Unwin Inc.,
9 Winchester Terrace, Winchester, Mass 01890, USA

George Allen & Unwin Australia Pty Ltd,
8 Napier Street, North Sydney, NSW 2060, Australia

First published in 1982

British Library Cataloguing in Publication Data

Le Grand, Julian
    The strategy of equality: redistribution and the
social services.
1. Public welfare – Great Britain – Finance
2. Equality   3. Social classes – Great Britain
305.5'0941   HM146
ISBN 0–04–336074–2
ISBN 0–04–336075–0 Pbk

Set in 11 on 12 point Times by Computacomp (UK) Ltd, Fort William, Scotland
and printed in Great Britain
by Biddles Ltd, Guildford, Surrey

Contents

List of Tables

List of Figures

To Polly and Zoe

Acknowledgements

I have had a great deal of help with this book. My biggest intellectual debt is to Ray Robinson who read an early draft of the whole manuscript and made innumerable useful suggestions for its improvement. I have had helpful comments on individual chapters from Brian Abel-Smith, Tony Atkinson, Nick Barr, Nick Bosanquet, Angela Coles, Stephen Glaister, John Jacobs, David Piachaud, George Psacharopoulos, Peter West, Christine Whitehead and David Winter. Richard Wilkinson provided biographical assistance for Chapter 3.

Over the years I have had a number of assistants who have worked on some of the research discussed in this book, among whom Fran Monk was particularly important. Dilia Montes helped with the final stages of the manuscript preparation and provided other assistance at crucial points. The staff of the London School of Economics and University of Sussex libraries were unfailingly courteous and helpful; I must mention, particularly, David Kennelly, Sheila Schaffer and Crispin Partridge for their patience with my endless requests over the years and their skill in meeting them. The Central Statistical Office and the Office of Population Censuses and Surveys gave me access to unpublished data; Susan Downing and Eileen Goddard of OPCS saved me from many mistakes in my interpretations of the results of the General Household Survey. My editor, Nicholas Brealey, made several suggestions for improving the book, and, despite considerable provocation due to my inability to meet deadlines, has been a continuous source of encouragement and support. Sue Kirkbride bore the brunt of the typing; a task she performed with fortitude and speed. Last, but not least, my wife has had to take on more than her share of family responsibilities, at a time when these were increasing dramatically, in order to allow me to finish the project. To them all, I am deeply grateful.

PART ONE

The Dream

CHAPTER 1

Introduction

The aim of this book is to examine a key element of what R. H. Tawney has termed the Strategy of Equality. This is the attempt to achieve social and economic equality through public spending on what are commonly termed the 'social services': health, education, housing and transport. Under this strategy the revenues raised through general taxation are used to fund the provision of these services free or at subsidised prices to some or all of those using them. By these means, it is believed the domain of inequality is severely restricted and its unfortunate social consequences eliminated.

This strategy has played a dominating role in the growth of public expenditure in Britain, and indeed throughout the world. Wholly or partially in the name of equality, most governments subsidise in some way the provision of medical care, education, housing and transport. Many also subsidise a wide variety of other goods and services for basically similar reasons. Yet there has been little analysis of these policies from an egalitarian point of view. Precisely what kind of equality is being aimed at? Does public expenditure on these goods and services actually achieve equality in any sense of the term? And what effect is there on the overall pattern of social and economic inequality? Despite the importance of such questions, few have tried to address them in any detail. Accordingly, this book is an attempt to rectify this omission.

Its conclusions are not comforting for those who subscribe to the strategy, or indeed for anyone who believes that public expenditure is broadly egalitarian in its effects. For the evidence reviewed suggests that:

● Almost all public expenditure on the social services in Britain benefits the better off to a greater extent than the poor. This is not only true for services such as roads where, due to the insignificant role played by a concern for equality in determining policy, such an outcome might be expected; it is also true for services whose aims are at least in part egalitarian, such as the National Health Service, higher education, public transport and the aggregate complex of housing policies.

- As a result equality, in any sense of the term, has not been achieved. In all the relevant areas, there persist substantial inequalities in public expenditure, in use, in opportunity, in access and in outcomes. Moreover, in some areas (though by no means all) there is evidence to suggest that the policies concerned have failed even to reduce inequality significantly.

The book's structure is straightforward. The next chapter outlines the Strategy of Equality, as expressed by its adherents, and endeavours to formalise it in as specific a fashion as possible. The next four chapters examine the distributional impact of public expenditure on health care, education, housing and transport: the key components of the 'social services' and essential elements of the Strategy of Equality. All these chapters have the same format. They begin with an investigation of the distribution of public expenditure in the area concerned, reviewing the available evidence, and, where relevant, discussing possible explanations for the distributional pattern that emerges. They continue with a brief consideration of the distribution of what might loosely be termed the 'outcome' of that expenditure: health standards, educational outcomes, housing conditions and travel. Where possible, the links between these distributions and the distribution of public expenditure in the area concerned are also examined. The final sections of each of these four chapters, entitled 'Equality and Policy', may be read independently of the other sections. They consist of a brief description of the various ways in which the objective of equality has been interpreted in the area concerned, an assessment as to whether equality, in any of its possible interpretations, has actually been achieved, and a discussion of the prospects for policy reform.

Chapter 7 draws on the material of the preceding four chapters to provide an overall assessment of this particular strategy of equality. Chapter 8 discusses an alternative strategy: the redistribution of money income. Finally, there are three appendices: Appendix A, which discusses studies of the distribution of public expenditure in general and some of the methodological difficulties they encounter; Appendix B, presenting some additional tables; and Appendix C, which describes the principal income and occupational classifications used in the main text.

The book may be read in a number of different ways, depending on the purpose of the reader. Those who want to know simply the main thrust of the argument should read Chapters 2, 7 and 8. Those interested in the individual services, but who are prepared to take the details of the statistics on trust, should look at the same three chapters, plus the sections on Equality and Policy in Chapters 3, 4, 5 and 6. And those whose concern is only with the facts concerning the distribution of public expenditure should read the first sections of Chapters 3, 4, 5 and 6, and Appendix A.

With the exception of Appendix A, technical terminology – whether of economists, sociologists or statisticians – has been avoided as far as possible, in order to make the book accessible to a wide audience. Those few technicalities that have crept into the main text are explained in notes at the end of each chapter. With the exception of certain government publications, which are referred to by their title, references to other work are signalled in the text by the name of the author followed by the date of publication: the full reference can be found in the Bibliography at the end of the book.

A final word. In some of what follows, extensive use is made of statistics. These are inhabitants of a cold realm; they lack the warmth of personal experience or the flow of bar-room anecdotes. Yet the facts they contain are essential; for no one individual's personal experience, however diverse, can equip him or her adequately to pass judgement on the consequences of a particular policy or set of policies. Every attempt has been made to make the numerical material as readable as possible; it is hoped that no one will find it too unpalatable.

CHAPTER 2

The Dreamers

> If every individual were reared in conditions as favourable
> to health as science can make them, received an equally
> thorough and stimulating education up to sixteen and knew
> on reaching manhood that ... he and his family could face
> the risks of life without being crushed by them, the most
> shocking of existing inequalities would be on the way to
> disappear ... Even inequalities in income ... would not
> continue in such conditions to be, either in magnitude or
> kind, what they are at present ... As ... the surplus elements
> in incomes were increasingly devoted to public purposes,
> while the means of health and education were equally
> diffused throughout the whole community, 'the career open
> to talent', which today is only a sham, would become a
> reality. *R. H. Tawney*

Large scale public spending is a relatively new phenomenon. In
the Middle Ages, virtually the only form of state expenditure was
military: the king funding his armies for the defence of the realm.
Even as late as 1890, total government expenditure comprised
less than a tenth of the Gross National Product (GNP) and nearly
half of that was on military and war-related items. But since that
time, public spending has increased dramatically. By 1900, it had
risen to 14 per cent of GNP; by 1920 it was over 25 per cent, and
by 1950 over 40 per cent. By 1978–9 total public expenditure was
over £70,000 million or 44 per cent of the national product.[1]

A large part of this growth was due to increased public
expenditure on what are generally described as the 'social
services'. In 1920 (the earliest date for which reliable data are
available) public expenditure on health care, education and
housing was less than 3 per cent of GNP: the proportion for
1978–9 was 15 per cent. If personal social services and transport

are included,[2] then total public expenditure on the social services in 1978–9 was £26,000 million or 18 per cent of GNP.

The importance of the social services relative to other areas of government expenditure can be gauged from Figure 2.1. This shows the relative sizes of different categories in 1978–9. After social security (which constituted a quarter of public expenditure in Great Britain in that year), education and health care were the biggest items in the government budget, taking up 13 and 11 per cent of public expenditure, respectively. After defence, housing was the next largest, with 8 per cent: transport and personal social services together took up 6 per cent. In total, expenditure on the social services comprised nearly 40 per cent of all government expenditure in Great Britain, and well over half of the expenditure on goods and services (public expenditure

Great Britain, 1978

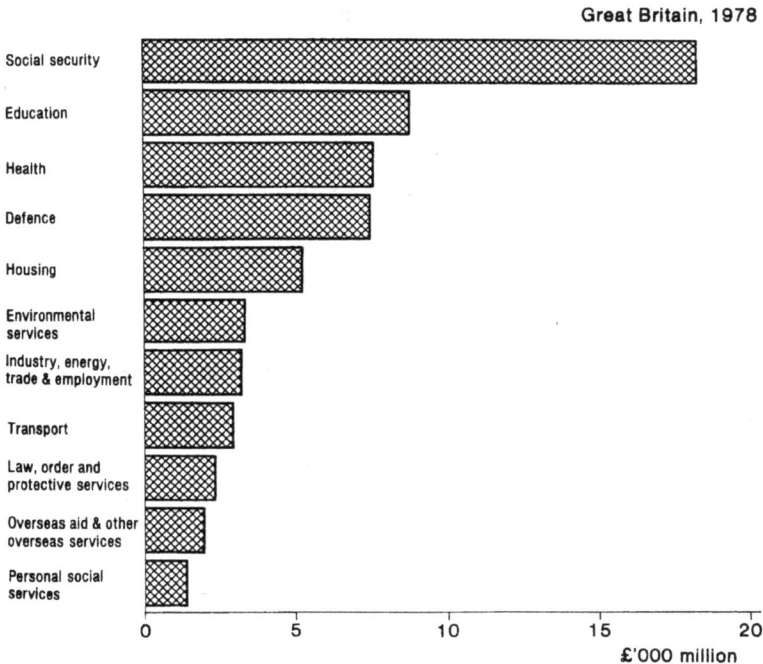

Figure 2.1   Public expenditure on selected services, Great Britain 1978–9.
Source: Appendix B, Table B.1.

excluding transfer payments, such as social security or debt interest).

A major justification for such a massive expansion of government activity has been the pursuit of equality. As will be illustrated in the first section of this chapter, the belief that some kind of equality can be achieved through public expenditure on the social services has long been an essential part of what R. H. Tawney called the Strategy of Equality. As will become apparent, it is widely believed that this strategy has actually been largely successful: that public expenditure in the relevant areas has indeed achieved a substantial measure of equality in some sense of the term. However, neither those who advocated the strategy nor those who believe it has worked have been very specific about the kind of equality they had (or have) in mind. Accordingly, the remainder of the chapter is an attempt to specify in as precise a fashion as possible the various ways in which the objective of equality can be interpreted, an essential preliminary to the analysis of the strategy's efficacy to be undertaken in subsequent chapters.

The Strategy of Equality

As the coiner of the phrase, Tawney should have the first word. An essential element of any strategy for reducing inequality, he argued, was (Tawney, 1964, p. 122):

> the pooling of [the nation's] resources by means of taxation, and the use of the funds thus obtained to make accessible to all, irrespective of their income, occupation, or social position, the conditions of civilization which, in the absence of such measures, can be enjoyed only by the rich.

By these means, he went on:

> It is possible for a society ... thus ... to abolish, if it pleases, the most crushing of the disabilities, and the most odious of the privileges which drive a chasm across it. It can secure that, in addition to the payments made to them for their labour, its citizens enjoy a social income ... [which] ... is available on equal terms for all its members.

The other major supporter of the strategy was Anthony Crosland. In the conclusion to his seminal work on egalitarian socialism (Crosland, 1956, p. 519) he emphasised that he laid:

> great stress on the relation, a direct and intimate one, between social expenditure and social equality. The former can promote the latter in two ways: first, by removing the greater handicap which poorer families suffer as compared with richer, during sickness, old age and the period of heaviest family responsibility, and secondly by creating standards of public health, education and housing which are comparable in scope and quality with the best available for private purchase.

The belief that public expenditure on the social services can promote social equality has not been confined to Tawney and Crosland. It has played a crucial role in the development of the welfare state in Britain (see, for example, Marshall, 1970, Ch. 12; Robson, 1976, Ch. II),[3] and it is now widely accepted that the aims of the social services include 'especially social equality' (Townsend, 1975, p. 28). It has had great influence on the Labour Party; for instance, the February 1974 manifesto included as one of its objectives: 'Increase social equality by giving far greater importance to full employment, *housing, education and social benefits*' (Craig, 1975, p. 405, emphasis added). In the United States it has become part of a philosophy, called variously 'specific egalitarianism' (Tobin, 1970) and 'categorical equity' (Feldstein, 1975), arguing that certain commodities should be distributed equally, or at least not according to individuals' ability to pay.

Nor does it lack support today. Dr David Owen, in his recent tract on social democracy, while also advocating the redistribution of private income and wealth, emphasises the importance of the 'social wage' as a means of attaining greater equality, and devotes much space to the ways in which policy in the relevant areas (housing, education and health care) can be reformed better to achieve that end (1981, pp. 97–110). Colin Crouch, in one of a recent collection of essays assembled as a tribute to Crosland, claims that 'it is impossible to envisage an egalitarian politics ... which will not need to divert resources from the unequal individualised market process so that they can be put to communal use by popularly responsive public agencies'

(1981, p. 185). Nïck Bosanquet, in the Fabian assessment of the 1974–9 Labour government's record in promoting equality, claims that 'it is hard to see how we can move towards a fairer society – a more even distribution of income and life chances – unless this core of the public sector [social security, education, the NHS, social services and housing] has an expanding share of GDP' (1980b, p. 40); although he goes on to add, in a significant caveat, that success would depend on how the money was used. And even such a fervent critic of egalitarianism as Sir Keith Joseph, in his polemic against equality written with Jonathan Sumption, has asserted that, if a society is unwise enough to attempt to promote equality, 'the only practical means of doing so' is via public spending on goods and services (Joseph and Sumption, 1979, p. 111).

The hope that equality of some kind can be attained through public expenditure' on the social services can also be found in statements, both official and unofficial, concerning the objectives of public policy towards specific services, particularly education and health care. Richard de Lone, in an important study for the Carnegie Council on Children, details how the belief in the egalitarian potential of education has dominated liberal efforts to obtain a more equal society in the United States (1979, Chs 1 and 2). Professor A. H. Halsey, one of Britain's foremost educational sociologists, has argued that a 'central theme of educational discussion from the beginning of the twentieth century' was the finding of 'a strategy for educational roads to equality' (1972, p. 3); and official documents produced under both Labour and Conservative governments on the objectives of education and health policy are replete with references to equality of one kind or another, as will be illustrated in subsequent chapters. Even in areas of public expenditure where equality is not always stated as an explicit objective, such as housing or transport, egalitarian aims are still present, usually expressed as a concern for 'fairness' or 'redistribution'.

This is not to imply that the attainment of equality is the sole aim of public expenditure on these services. It has often been argued that some state intervention in these areas is justified in order to promote a more efficient functioning of the economy (see Le Grand and Robinson, 1976, especially Chapters 2, 3, 4 and 6). Perhaps more importantly for the purposes of this book there are aspects of policy which seem to be aimed at attaining a *minimum standard* below which no one should fall, rather than equality as such. This was clearly what Sir William Beveridge had in mind when he stated in his famous Report on Social Security that the aim of social expenditure was to ensure 'Freedom from Want' (*Social Insurance and Allied Services*, pp. 7–9); and some kind of minimum standards objective seems to be implied in official statements concerning, particularly, housing and transport. Even Crosland at one point argues that 'the ultimate purpose of the social services ... must surely be the relief of social distress and hardship, and the correction of social need', although, he went on to add, 'naturally measures directed to this end will often enhance social equality, which in any case remains an important subsidiary objective' (1956, p. 148).

But two points should be made in this connection. First, the minimum standard objective does not seem to have influenced policy towards some of the social services, at least to the same extent as the more comprehensive egalitarian objectives. As T. H. Marshall argued in his essay on Citizenship and Social Class: 'the aim of social rights' (in which he included the public provision of health, education and housing) 'is no longer merely an attempt to abate the obvious notion of destitution in the lowest ranks of society. It has assumed the guise of action modifying the whole pattern of social inequality' (1963, p. 100). And in his textbook on the welfare state J. F. Sleeman (1973, p. 5) states that:

> We now accept that ... not only should the Government provide social services, such as social security, medical treatment, education, welfare facilities and subsidized housing, but these should go beyond the provision of a bare minimum towards ensuring that all have equal opportunity, so far as the country's resources allow.

Second, the objectives of minimum standards and equality cannot easily be divorced. For the level at which a minimum is set will depend on the levels that prevail elsewhere in the society. As a result, policies intended to raise people above a minimum standard without having any effect on inequality are likely to be self-defeating. For if everyone's standards are raised so as to ensure that no one falls below a given minimum, while at the same time preserving relative inequalities, the notion of what constitutes the acceptable 'floor' will also rise, thus making it likely that there will still be some people below the minimum. Hence a policy ostensibly concerned only with minimum standards will perforce also have to be concerned with equality.

Overall, it seems clear that there is a widespread belief that public expenditure on the social services can promote equality and that this belief has played a major role in guiding public policy in those areas. Since most of these policies have now been in existence for considerable periods of time, the obvious questions arise: Have they had the desired effect? Have the relevant inequalities been eliminated? Has the Strategy of Equality worked?

Many believe that the answer to all these questions is yes; equality, in one sense or another, has been achieved. In particular, it is widely believed that public expenditure on the social services has been directed at the less well off, that such expenditures benefit the poor more than the rich. For instance, in a critique of the cuts in taxation and public expenditure that are currently taking place in Britain, J. K. Galbraith recently argued that 'the major benefit of tax reduction is for the affluent: the curtailment of services and welfare – hospitals, schools, libraries, police services, housing – is most noticed by the poor'.[4] Further to the right of the political spectrum, Sir Keith Joseph has claimed that 'public assets and public expenditure are distributed either equally or else in favour of those who do badly in comparisons of private wealth holdings' (Joseph and Sumption, 1979, p. 110). J. F. Sleeman argues that: 'the British Welfare State, in spite of its deficiencies, has done quite a lot to redistribute command over goods and services in favour of those whose need is greatest, the lowest income groups and the large families. This is done mainly through the incidence of the benefits of expenditure on social services in cash *and kind*' (1973, p. 121, emphasis added).

A belief that public expenditure benefits the poor is also an essential component of some of the theories put forward by social scientists to explain the development of the welfare state. For instance, it plays an important role in some Marxist analyses of the phenomenon. There, the provision of social services is simply one of the tools by which the state achieves its primary purpose – that of serving the interests of the capitalist class. It does this in two ways: by increasing the quantity and quality of the labour force ('the reproduction of labour power') and by maintaining social harmony ('the reproduction of the relations of production').

State expenditure on education, for instance, both improves the productivity of the labour force, and also inculcates the values and beliefs necessary for the continuance of capitalist society. Public health care improves the productivity of the labour force and, by alleviating the misery of ill-health, defuses a possible source of social tension. Public housing reduces the discontent of the labour force, promotes its health and also, by preserving the power imbalances inevitable in the landlord/tenant relationship, manages to reproduce the relations of the productive system.

This is not the place for a detailed discussion of this thesis. Rather, it is one of its empirical foundations that is of interest, viz., the implied requirement that the working class are the prime recipients of public expenditure. All the arguments mentioned above require this to be true; indeed, Ian Gough (1979, pp. 108–17), in his critique of the welfare state from a Marxist perspective, quotes Central Statistical Office data showing a supposed pro-poor distribution of the social services to buttress his argument.

The view is also implicit in another theory explaining the development of the welfare state – in particular, public expenditure on social services – often put forward by economists.[5] This hypothesises that taxpayers have an altruistic but paternalistic concern for the welfare of the less well off. That is, they are prepared to vote (and to pay) for some kind of redistribution to the poor, but only if it takes the form of providing them with specific commodities such as health care or education. This is because taxpayers do not trust the poor to spend any extra income 'wisely': hence they prefer to give aid in kind rather than aid in cash. Again, the validity of this theory depends on this redistribution in kind actually being in favour of the poor; for if it is not, the policies concerned will not attract voter support, and therefore will not be instituted.

The belief that public expenditure on social services benefits primarily the less well off is thus widespread. Yet there have been curiously few attempts to establish whether this really is the case. Nor have there been many serious efforts to discover whether such public expenditure achieves equality in any other sense of the term. This may be in part because in order properly to assess whether or not a particular policy has achieved an objective, it is necessary to specify precisely what that objective is. But, as has already become apparent, egalitarian aims can be phrased in a variety of ways, none of which are notable for their precision. In particular two questions have to be sorted out: Equality of what? and Equality between whom? Possible answers to these questions are discussed in the next two sections.

Equality of What?

There seem to be five distinct types of equality that appear in one context or another as suitable objectives for guiding the distribution of public expenditure. The first is *equality of public expenditure*. Public expenditure on the provision of a particular social service should be allocated equally between all relevant individuals. Although this aim is rarely stated explicitly, it underlies many of the controversies, both old and new, over actual distributive outcomes; for instance, those concerning the relative sizes of the public subsidies to owner occupiers and council tenants, imbalances between regions in hospital spending and in differences in public expenditure between types of school.

The second type might be termed *equality of final income*. Public expenditure on the social services should be allocated in such a way as to favour the poor, so that their 'final incomes' (roughly, private money income plus the value of any public subsidy received in cash or in kind[6]) are brought more into line with those of the rich. The belief that this is a suitable aim for public expenditure on the social services is a common one, being implicit, for instance, in the widely held view that such expenditure should be (and is) 'redistributive'.

The third type may be termed *equality of use*. Public expenditure on a social service should be allocated so that the amounts of the service used by all relevant individuals are the same. An example of an objective of this type may be found in the objective often ascribed to the National Health Service: equal treatment for equal need. Here the relevant individuals are those in similar states of ill-health. Another example is a definition of equality of educational opportunity that underlies much contemporary thinking on educational policy: viz. that, on average, members of each social category (race, sex, class or whatever) should receive similar amounts of education (Halsey, 1972, p. 8). Here the relevant individuals are the 'average' members of different social categories.

A fourth objective, somewhat different from the others, is *equality of cost*. Public expenditure should be allocated in such a way that all relevant individuals face the same private cost per 'unit' of the service used. For instance, the cost to an individual of consulting a doctor, or of spending an extra year in school, should be the same for all individuals. The cost could be taken to mean the expenditure of money and/or time; or it could be interpreted more broadly as the welfare or satisfaction forgone through that expenditure. Although this conception may at first sight seem unfamiliar, I believe it to be the kernel of the more well known, but less well defined, notion of 'equality of access' that appears frequently in connection with health care and education. The requirement that all individuals should have equal access to a service can be most easily interpreted as implying that the costs to all individuals of using that service (per unit) should be equal; for if two individuals wishing to use the service face different costs of doing so, then access to the service is surely unequal.

The fifth type of equality is *equality of outcome*. Public expenditure should be allocated so as to promote equality in the 'outcome' associated with a particular service. Precisely what is meant by outcome will vary from service to service. For health care it could be an individual's state of health; for education, the bundle of skills with which an individual emerges from the education system; the extra income which he can earn as a result of his education; for housing, the conditions of individuals' dwellings; for transport, personal mobility or travel. This objective has been particularly important in the case of education; for, as noted earlier, the belief that education could be used as a means of obtaining a more equal society (in terms of income or social mobility) has been a crucial influence on social policy in the area.

It should be noted that it is not possible in every case to distinguish easily between the use of a service and its outcome; in particular, education and housing present problems. In the case of education, the use of successive stages of the education system could be viewed as the outcome of the previous stages, since progress up the system depends on earlier prowess. For housing, the service and the outcome merge, as the services provided or subsidised by public expenditure on housing are the dwellings themselves. In what follows, therefore, no distinction is drawn between use and outcome in the housing case; and in education the slightly arbitrary distinction is made that continuation in the education system constitutes use, while educational performance in examinations, etc., constitutes (part of) outcome.

So there appear to be at least five different kinds of equality underlying policy towards public expenditure on the social services. One way of judging the effectiveness of such policy is therefore to assess whether full equality, in any of its different manifestations, has been achieved in the areas concerned; and this will indeed be a principal concern of subsequent chapters. Another, less stringent, test is to ask not whether *full* equality has been achieved but rather just *greater* equality. This is perhaps a fairer test, particularly in the case of final income since it is unlikely that even the most fervent advocate of the egalitarian potential of public spending on the social services believes that it could completely offset inequalities in private incomes. However, it is much more difficult to put into practice; for it immediately raises the question, greater equality than what? Some point of comparison has to be established, some distribution against which the observed distribution can be compared. Two possible candidates for such a distribution are the distribution of the relevant indicator (expenditure, final income, use, cost or outcome) that pertained in the relevant area in the past, and the distribution that would pertain in the present if current policies were withdrawn (or altered in some way). The first is easier to implement than the second. There is no difficulty in principle in comparing a distribution in the present with one in the past – although, of course, in practice data difficulties may impede the procedure. Accordingly, attempts are made to do this in the relevant chapters, wherever the data permit.

The second case, however, raises deeper issues. For it requires predicting all the relevant changes that would occur if a particular area of public expenditure were eliminated. For instance, suppose one wished to test the proposition that 'the National Health Service has created greater equality than would otherwise exist'. In order to undertake properly such a test, it would be necessary to establish what system of medical care would replace it if it were abolished; what would happen to taxation; what would be the effect on personal incomes, and so on. Then it would be necessary to predict the distributions in the new situation of public expenditure, of health care, of costs, of health and of final income – all in all, an enormously difficult task and one that would involve an enormous amount of guesswork, much of which would be unlikely to command general assent. Accordingly, no detailed attempt to make such a comparison is made in any of the chapters dealing with specific areas of public expenditure; however, the issue is addressed in a broader context in Chapter 7.

Equality between Whom?

The principal focus of the strategists of equality was the differences that exist between social groups defined in terms of social class. Crosland repeatedly states that his ideal is one of a 'classless' society (1956, pp. 67, 76–7). Tawney was yet more explicit, writing (1964, pp. 57–8):

> In communities no longer divided by religion or race, and in which men and women are treated as political and economic equals, the divisions which remain are, nevertheless, not insignificant. The practical form which they most commonly assume – the most conspicuous external symptom of differences of economic status and social position – is, of course, a graduated system of social classes, and it is by softening or obliterating, not individual differences, but class gradations that the historical movements directed towards diminishing inequality have attempted to attain their objective.

It is now clear that Tawney was rather too optimistic about the attainment of equality between individuals of different races and between men and women. However, most distributional studies have concentrated upon the differences between groups defined in terms of their social or economic status using indicators such as occupation or income, an emphasis which inevitably has therefore dominated this book.

Conclusion

A major objective underlying the (considerable) growth in public expenditure in the social services has been that of equality. But the kinds of equality envisaged have not been uniform. Five different types have been distinguished: equality of public expenditure, final income, use, cost and outcome. Many people believe that, in at least one or more of these interpretations, equality has indeed been achieved through public expenditure on the social services. Part Two attempts to assess whether this belief is well-founded.

The four chapters in Part Two examine health care, education, housing and transport, respectively. Unfortunately, there is no statistical evidence concerning the distributional impact of the personal social services, which have therefore had to be excluded.[7] Each chapter investigates the evidence concerning the distribution of public expenditure, final income, use, costs and outcomes between various social groupings in the area concerned. By and large the evidence refers to Britain, although studies for other countries are mentioned where relevant. Public expenditure is interpreted as including not only direct expenditures of the normal kind, but also 'tax expenditures', that is, tax reliefs associated with various of the services (such as owner-occupied housing) which depress the government's revenue and thus have exactly the same effect on its budget as if the individuals concerned had received a direct grant from the government. The social groups are defined in terms of income or occupation; details of the principal classifications employed may be found in Appendix C. Each chapter concludes with a section which summarises the evidence, discusses the implications for equality and reviews the possibilities for policy reform.

Notes to Chapter 2

1   All figures in this chapter are calculated from either Peacock and Wiseman (1961) or Appendix B, Table B.1.
2   Personal social services includes the provision of residential care for children, the elderly and the mentally handicapped, and the activities of non-residential social workers. Transport includes both public transport and private transport (particularly the private car); in general, only the first is considered as a 'social service' but, as will be apparent in Chapter 6, it is difficult to consider public expenditure on one separately from that on the other.
3   For an apparently contrary view, see Wilensky (1975) who, in a statistical study across a wide variety of countries, found that indicators of an ideological commitment to equality played no role in explaining variations in spending across the countries investigated. However, this does not imply

that the *growth* in such spending cannot be explained (at least in part) by such a commitment.

4 *The Observer*, 31 August, 1980.
5 For examples and references, see Collard (1978, pp. 122–3).
6 A more formal definition can be found in Appendix C.
7 For some discussion of the relationship between equality and the personal social services, see Webb (1980).

PART TWO

The Reality

CHAPTER 3

Health Care

> The Government ... want to ensure that in future every man, woman and child can rely on getting all the advice and treatment and care which they may need in matters of personal health; that what they get shall be the best medical and other facilities available; that their getting these shall not depend on whether they can pay for them, or any other factor irrelevant to the real need. *A National Health Service*, Cmd 6502

Health affects every aspect of life. Our ability to work, to play, to enjoy our families or to socialise with friends, all depend crucially upon our physical well-being. Serious illnesses create enormous pain and suffering; even minor, transient ailments can be depressing psychologically as well as debilitating physically. And ill-health which leads to death makes all other sources of satisfaction irrelevant.

So it is not surprising that health care is a major focus for social concern. Every Western government has intervened to a greater or lesser extent in the provision of health care, ranging from the broad national health insurance schemes of France and West Germany to the more selective US programmes of Medicare (for the old) and Medicaid (for the poor). But few have a system as comprehensive as the British National Health Service (NHS), a scheme whereby most forms of medical care are provided free (or largely free) at the time of use to anyone who is judged to need it. The NHS is now the third largest item of government expenditure in Great Britain; in 1978–9 it cost over £7,500 million, or 11 per cent of total public spending.[1]

That the distribution of health care should not be left to the operations of the private market is a view that is widely shared. Market allocation has been described as socially inefficient, as damaging the doctor/patient relationship and as reducing the scope for altruistic behaviour.[2] But a major justification for state intervention has been the attainment of some kind of equality. Equality of treatment, equality of access and equality of health itself, these and other conceptions of equality dominate official and unofficial statements concerning the objectives of the NHS. It is therefore important to establish whether it has actually achieved equality in any of its manifestations; and it is this issue to which this chapter is addressed.[3] The first section discusses the available evidence concerning the distribution of public expenditure on health care and considers possible explanations for that distribution. The second examines the evidence concerning the distribution of health itself, and discusses its relationship to the distribution of health care. Finally, the third section relates the actual distributions to the possible objectives of equality and discusses policy changes that might bring one into line with the other.

The Distribution of Public Expenditure

A breakdown of public expenditure on health care in Britain for 1978–9 is given in Figure 3.1. By far the largest proportion goes towards hospital and community health services, comprising about 75 per cent of the total (capital plus current). Of the remainder, about 6 per cent goes on the services of general practitioners (GPs), 3 per cent on dental services, 11 per cent on pharmaceuticals and 5 per cent on ophthalmic and central health services.

There have been no published studies of the distribution of this expenditure by income group that are based on actual surveys of use.[4] However, the present author undertook an investigation of the distribution by socio-economic group (SEG) based on the General Household Survey (GHS). This is a continuous survey of some 32,000 people carried out by the Office of Population Censuses and Surveys (OPCS) every year since 1971. Among other things, it asks questions concerning respondents' states of health and their utilisation of the Health Service. In particular, until 1976 respondents were asked whether they suffered any 'acute' sickness (illness that restricted their activity in the last two weeks) or 'chronic' sickness (long-standing illness that limited

CURRENT

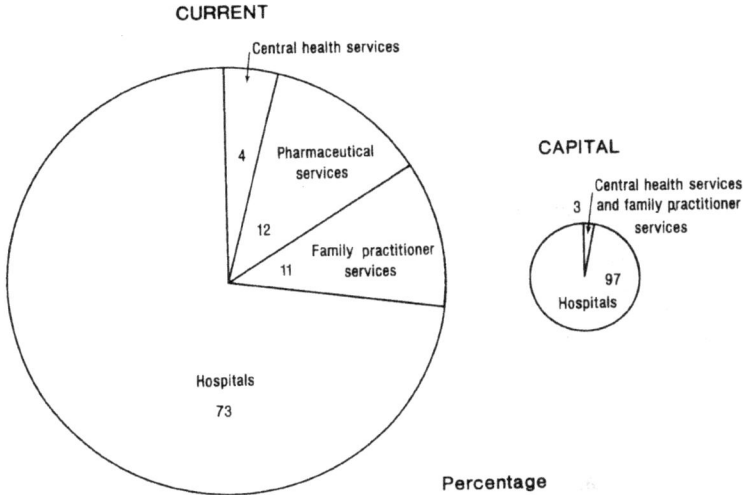

Figure 3.1 Public expenditure on health care by category, Great Britain 1978–9.
Source: Appendix B, Table B.2.

their activity); they were also asked for the number of GP and hospital out-patient consultations made and the length of time spent as a hospital in-patient, within particular reference periods.

The study concerned (Le Grand, 1978) used 1972 GHS data on utilisation and official estimates of the current cost to the NHS of each 'unit' of utilisation (i.e. the cost per doctor and hospital out-patient consultation and per hospital in-patient day) to calculate the total cost of the health service resources (excluding capital) used by each group.[5] These figures were then divided by the numbers of persons reporting illness (acute, chronic or both) in each group to obtain the NHS expenditure per person in 'need' of health care. They could also have been divided by the total numbers of persons in each group (ill and not ill) to obtain the average expenditure per person for each group; although this was not done in the original study, it has been for this book and both sets of results are presented in Table 3.1.

From the second column of this table, it is apparent that there is no consistent pattern favouring either the higher or the lower SEGs in so far as expenditure per person is concerned. But if differences

Table 3.1   *Public Expenditure on Health Care by
Socio-Economic Group*

All persons		*England and Wales 1972*
Socio-economic group	*Expenditure per person: percentage of mean*	*Expenditure per person reporting illness: percentage of mean*
Professionals, employers and managers	94	120
Intermediate and junior non-manual	104	114
Skilled manual	92	97
Semi- and unskilled manual	114	85
Mean (£) = 100	18.1	103.2

Source: Calculated as in Le Grand (1978).

in need are taken into account a rather different picture emerges. The third column shows that public expenditure per person reporting illness is greater, the higher the social group. The differences between the top and bottom are considerable, with the highest group (professional, employers, managers and their families) receiving over 40 per cent more than the lowest group (semi-skilled and unskilled manual workers and their families). It appears that across SEGs, NHS expenditure per unit of need is quite unequal.

These results could be challenged on a number of grounds. First, some of the utilisation data (particularly for hospital in-patients) were based on very small samples. Second, there are problems with reported illness as an indicator of actual ill-health and hence of 'need'. But, as is argued in the next section, there are good reasons to suppose that reported illness is the best of the available indicators; moreover, since the other indicators show a similar distribution to reported illness, the use of any one of them instead would not alter the broad pattern of the results. Third, it might be claimed that the results are an artefact of some kind: that they derive simply from differences in the age and sex composition of the groups. However, standardising the results for such differences that exist between the groups made little difference to the overall inequality.

` A more serious difficulty concerns one of the assumptions on which the calculations were based. It was assumed that the resource cost per 'unit' of utilisation was the same, regardless of SEG. A Scottish Home and Health Department study (Buchan and Richardson, 1973) found that doctors spent on average one-and-a-half times as long with their patients from Social Class I as with their patients from Social Class V. An investigation of doctor consultations with ninety-two elderly patients in England and Wales reported similar findings (Cartwright and O'Brien, 1976). Although the grouping of occupations by social class is not the same as that by SEG (see Appendix C) the top and bottom of both classifications broadly correspond to one another. Hence it seems reasonable to suppose that the cost of the average GP consultation made by an individual from the higher SEG is greater than the equivalent for the lower ones. Probably the same is true for out-patient consultations and in-patient hospital data; for, just as with doctors, middle-class patients will be better able to direct the resources of a hospital towards their needs than working-class patients. Hence it is probable that the figures in Table 3.1 actually *under*estimate the true degree of inequality in NHS provision.

Now there are two possible explanations for the inequality revealed in the figures. The first is that it reflects the fact that the higher SEGs have different diseases from the lower ones; diseases which are significantly more expensive to treat. Unfortunately, this 'fact' has little to support it. Such evidence as does exist (again from the GHS) suggests that the distribution of disease is remarkably uniform across socio-economic groups. The lower groups have a substantially higher incidence of almost all forms of sickness than the higher ones; but, since they also report more sickness overall, the *proportions* of those reporting illness in each group who have a particular disease are largely identical (Le Grand, 1978, pp. 134–6).

The second explanation for the unequal expenditure is that there exist substantial differences in the use of the Health Service between the groups, at least in relation to their health. People in the lower SEGs appear prepared to report themselves as ill to a General Household Survey interviewer, but not to go to the doctor – or, more accurately, not to use the facilities of the Health Service to the same extent as their counterparts in the higher groups. This is borne out by a number of other studies. The National Child Development Study found that children up to the age of 7 in Social Class I, compared with those in Social Class V, were twice as likely to have visited a dentist, and five, ten and eleven times as likely to have been vaccinated against smallpox, polio and diphtheria, respectively (Central Statistical Office, 1975, p. 27, Table 7.5). Donald Forster, of the Department of Community Medicine at the University of Sheffield, used GHS data on doctor consultations and reported sickness to calculate use/need ratios for different SEGs (1976). He found that these increased with SEG: that is, the higher groups used the health service more relative to their needs than the lower ones. M. Alderson (1970) reported on several separate examples of inequalities in the use of health services by social class. He found that, with respect to mass radiography, cervical screening, pregnancy and infant care, dental treatment, breast operations and hospital referrals, use in relation to need was highest among Social Classes I and II and lowest among Social Classes IV and V. He concluded (Alderson, 1970, p. 52):

> The data presented are compatible with the hypothesis that there is a group in the community who are aware of the provisions of the health service and who obtain a higher proportion of the resources of the health service than would be expected by chance, and a much higher proportion in relation to their needs when compared with others in the community.

The recent report of the working party on inequalities in health chaired by Sir Douglas Black reviewed the evidence and came to similar conclusions (Black, 1980, pp. 116–18). Cartwright and O'Brien (1976, p. 93) in another review summarised their overall impressions as follows:

> There appears to us to be fairly conclusive evidence that the middle class made more use of preventive services. There is also enough evidence to suggest that the middle class may, in relation to a number of services, receive better care.

Recently some evidence has emerged that at first sight seems to yield different conclusions. In the 1977 and 1978 General Household Surveys the questions concerning health were changed. In particular, people who reported themselves as having some health problems were asked if they had contacted the health services about them. The results showed that the lower groups contacted the health service more – in relation to need – than the higher ones. More specifically, the proportion of all those who reported chronic health problems and who had some contact with the health service in both the year before interview and in the two weeks before interview was greater for the lower SEGs. A similar pattern appeared for the proportion of males (though not for females) reporting short-term health problems who contacted a doctor in the two weeks before interview.[6]

Elizabeth Collins and Rudolf Klein (1980) of the University of Bath have taken the matter further. They used 1974 GHS data on use of the NHS broken down by the state of reported health, as well as by age and socio-economic group. 'Use' was defined as one or more visits to a GP in a two-week reference period; the health groups were those reporting acute sickness, chronic sickness without restrictions of normal activity, chronic sickness with some restriction, and those reporting no sickness at all. They found the only consistent class gradient that favoured the top SEGs was for males in the 'not-sick' group. The gradients for females in that category, and for both males and females in all three of the 'sick' groups, were either inconsistent or favoured the lower SEGs.

How may these results be reconciled with the evidence discussed earlier? Collins and Klein appear to believe that all the published estimates used the same unit of 'use' as they do, viz., one or more contacts with a GP, and therefore explain the differences between the previous results and theirs by the inclusion in the former of figures of use by those who are not sick. Eileen Goddard of OPCS has suggested a similar explanation for the GHS results.[7] Use by the non-sick may indeed be part of the explanation, but it is unlikely to be a very important one. Collins and Klein found only a small class gradient in the not-sick category, and that only for males. Since in their sample male not-sick users comprised less than 15 per cent of all users, it seems unlikely that this small gradient would be sufficient to outweigh the neutral or pro-lower SEG gradients they found in other categories – certainly not to the extent of creating the substantial inequality revealed in the earlier results.

Apart from the ever present danger of sampling error, the only other possible explanation for the disparity is that there exist substantial differences between SEGs in the *extent* of NHS contact, differences which the estimates of the distribution of public expenditure capture (albeit imperfectly) but which Collins and Klein and the GHS reports do not. That such differences exist has scattered support from independent sources. Backett (1977, p. 119) refers to a study showing that 'upper class patients were referred more frequently to hospital than lower class ones. The study was based on a random sample of general practitioners and the finding referred only to the *second* doctor–patient contact in an episode of illness' (emphasis in the original). A study by Cartwright mentioned in the Black report (1980, pp. 104–5) showed that women from Social Class V received the lowest degree of intensive care during their pregnancies, and were very much less likely to have their babies induced in hospital; and there is evidence to show that home visits by consultants to patients in terminal care favoured the higher social classes (Backett, 1977, p. 119).

Moreover, there is a relatively simple explanation for some of the high first contact results reported by Collins and Klein and the GHS. This is the need for sickness absence certificates, a need which does not necessarily lead to substantial subsequent contact and which is concentrated largely in the lower occupational groups. That this may be the correct explanation for the anomaly can be inferred from the fact that in Collins's and Klein's results, the only significant pro-lower SEG results are those for males who are acutely sick (a phenomenon which they themselves partly attribute to the need for sickness certificates). Similarly, the GHS results show that for short-term health problems (the ones most likely to require a medical certificate) the consistent trend of greater contact by the lower social groups is true only for males. Indeed, in so far as there is any trend, it is reversed for females, with the exception of those in the families of unskilled manual workers which happens to be the group with the largest proportion of working women.

Despite appearances, therefore, this new evidence does not directly contradict the old. In particular, the conclusion derived from the earlier evidence remains intact: that the better off appear to receive more health care under the NHS relative to need than the less well off. This also appears to have been the experience of the public health care systems of other countries. In the United States, Part B of the Medicare programme finances a large proportion of health treatment for the elderly, including all physician services, X-rays and laboratory tests, ambulance services and home health care. A study of its distribution by

Karen Davis and Roger Reynolds (1975) found that those with incomes of over $15,000 per annum derived over twice as much benefit per person eligible as those with incomes under $5,000. The Medicaid programme provides free care to low-income families, and, as such, of course, largely benefits the poor as a group. But *within* that group there are substantial differences in benefit, again favouring the better off (Davis, 1977). Meerman (1979) and Selowsky (1979), in their studies of the (very different) public health systems of Malaysia and Colombia, concluded in each case that public expenditure was distributed equally between income groups, a conclusion which implies that, since ill-health is almost certainly concentrated in the poorer groups, public expenditure per ill person is unequal.

What of changes over time? There is no evidence concerning the distribution of public expenditure (or any useful proxy) on health care prior to the introduction of the National Health Service. However, it is likely that it was concentrated largely upon the worse off. As Brian Abel-Smith has noted, 'the working class could ... get ... free ... health services before the war. The contributor to National Health Insurance had the services of a panel doctor and anyone who was poor could go to a voluntary or local authority hospital without any payment'. As a result, he went on, 'the main effect of the post-war development of the social services [such as the NHS] ... has been to provide free social services to the middle classes' (1958, pp. 56–7).

The NHS, therefore, along with other systems of public health care, appears to favour the better off. This raises the obvious question: Why? Why do those lower down the social scale use the NHS less (relative to their need) than their middle-class counterparts, even though the majority of its services are provided free? Or, put another way, why are there differences in the demand for health care between individuals in different social groups?

An individual's demand for health care has two sources: the individual him- or herself, and the suppliers of that care. That is, individuals may make the original decision to contact the health service, but, once they have done so, many of the subsequent decisions about how much care they will receive will be out of their hands. General practitioners make decisions concerning referrals to specialists; specialists make decisions about stays in hospital; home visits by medical practitioners or health visitors are made largely at their own discretion. Hence individual differences in the use of services may spring from either or both of two sources: differences in the basic demand by the relevant individuals and differences in demand induced by the suppliers of medical care themselves.

Consider first differences in the demand by individuals. Here it is helpful to use a rational model of individual behaviour commonly employed by economists. Although some may be put off by the terminology, such a model is extremely simple and, at its most general level, almost uncontrovertible. All that is required is the assumption that, in deciding whether or not to use a particular 'unit' of health care (such as a visit to the doctor or an out-patient consultation), individuals weigh up the costs and benefits of the unit concerned. The benefits will be any improvement in their health which they perceive as following from their use of the particular unit. The costs (in the case of free provision) will be primarily those of time; time spent travelling to the medical facility concerned, time spent waiting for treatment having once arrived (including waiting in a hospital bed) and time spent on actual treatment. If, in any given situation, the benefits outweigh the costs, the individual will use the unit concerned; conversely, if the costs outweigh the benefits, he or she will not use it.

Simple as this 'model' is, it is a powerful tool for improving our understanding of the factors affecting differential use of medical services since these factors can be usefully divided into those affecting costs and those affecting benefits. As far as costs are concerned, there are several reasons why the costs of using a free service will be greater for potential working class users from the lower SEGs than for those from the higher ones. Time spent travelling will be greater because they are more reliant upon public transport (in 1976, under a third of semi- and unskilled manual workers' households had cars compared with nearly 90 per cent of those of professionals[8]). Also, they are likely to have further to travel, for the areas in which they live are poorly endowed with medical facilities (Noyce, Snaith and Trickey, 1974; Backett, 1977, pp. 111–12). The costs of waiting are likely to be higher, since they cannot so easily make appointments by telephone (a quarter of unskilled manual workers' households in 1976 had telephones compared with nearly 90 per cent of those of professionals, employers and managers[9]).

Not only may the lower groups lose more time using the NHS than the higher ones, but the cost of each hour thus lost may be greater, particularly for those in work. Many professionals and managers are paid an annual salary and hence are unlikely to lose income for time spent visiting the doctor during working hours, whereas workers in manual occupations, paid by the day or the hour, may have to forgo their pay for any time thus taken off. Cartwright (1964) found that during a spell in hospital only 20 per cent of working-class heads of household received full wages, compared with nearly 80 per cent of middle-class ones. Indeed, over half the working-class heads of households received no money at all from their employers, compared with just 12 per cent of those of the middle class. (It must be added that if they *do* lose money, middle-class workers are likely to lose more, as their wage rates are generally higher. But even then the actual sacrifice involved may be less, for each pound of loss is likely to involve a greater sacrifice for those on lower incomes than for those on higher incomes.)

Not only costs but the perceptions of the benefits from health care may differ between the groups. This may be because the health knowledge of the lower groups is poorer in some respects (for instance, they may know less about preventive services). But it may also be because the benefits *are* rather less. Individuals from lower social groups can find the Health Service – staffed as it is with largely middle-class personnel – as at best unhelpful and at worst actively hostile to their interests. Immigrant groups, in particular, may encounter actual discrimination.

There is evidence to support the view that there are considerable problems of communication between working-class patients and doctors. In the survey of elderly patients mentioned above, the researchers found (Cartwright and O'Brien, 1976, p. 94):

General practitioners knew more about the domestic situation of their middle class patients, although working class patients had been with them for longer. Middle-class patients discussed more problems and spent longer in conversation with the doctor. They may also ask more questions and get more information.

That all these factors are important in explaining the differential use of the Health Service receives support from an interesting study (Earthrowl and Stacey, 1977) on a related subject: the visiting of children in hospital. A survey of 1,000 children discharged from Welsh hospitals in 1972 found that working-class parents visited their children less frequently than middle-class parents.[10] The explanation for this was not because of a lack of concern by the working-class parents for their children. Indeed, beliefs as to what would be best for their children in terms of visiting, giving information and so on were virtually identical to those of the middle-class parents. Rather, the reasons were essentially the ones discussed above. A quarter of the working-class respondents found just simply obtaining transport to visit their children very or quite difficult, while nearly half found *paying* for it a hardship. Moreover, the working-class parents, when they did arrive, were treated differently by the hospital staff from the middle-class parents, resulting in their finding out less about their child's treatment and the facilities available.

More support comes from US studies. For instance, Davis (1977, pp. 202–3) concluded with respect to the Medicaid programme:

> Medicaid ... has been most beneficial to those able to seek out and obtain appropriate medical care. For those poor persons facing significant nonfinancial barriers to medical care – such as limited availability of services, transportation handicaps, or discrimination – benefits have been much lower.

Costs greater, benefits lower: it is not surprising that the lower social groups demand less medical care than the higher ones, even when there is no charge. But the explanation for the distribution does not stop there. The differences in original demand may be reinforced by differences in the second determinant of overall demand, that which is supplier induced. It has already been mentioned that there is evidence showing that upper-class patients are referred by their GPs more frequently to hospital than those from the lower class. Other studies have shown, *inter alia*, that middle-class patients had fewer doctor-induced delays in obtaining abortions (Backett, 1977, p. 119) and that health visitors may visit middle-class households more relative to need than working-class ones (Black, 1980, p. 108). Although far from comprehensive, such findings are suggestive; at the least, it would appear that differences in supplier-induced demand cannot be ruled out as an essential part of the explanation for the inequalities being examined.

The Distribution of Health

An essential preliminary to any examination of the distribution of health or ill-health is to decide upon how 'health' is to be measured. What constitutes good health? How would we decide whether one individual is healthier than another? What indicators can be found that would permit the ranking of different classes according to their states of health?

This is a problem with a long history. In 1911, the Registrar General produced mortality (or death) rates for different social classes in an effort to emphasise the health differences between occupational groups (in fact, it was for this purpose that the Registrar General's social class groupings were devised); and since then comparisons of mortality rates have become a standard way of comparing the health of different groups. But other indicators have also been used. These include evidence from medical records, days off sick and illness as reported directly by people interviewed in sample surveys.

All have their disadvantages. Mortality rates are not necessarily good indicators of general health, since not all illness is fatal. Medical records have the advantage of being informed by expert knowledge but they are often incomplete and, for confidentiality reasons, are not easily consulted. They also ignore any illness that does not come to the attention of the health care system – an omission which may be of considerable importance. Days off sick can be more easily obtained (from sample surveys or from examination of national insurance certificates), but, given the wide variety of reasons why people take the day off, may not be very reliable. With the institution in the early 1970s of the General Household Survey there is now available a lot of information on illness as reported directly by households. But this may not be wholly reliable, either, not because of malingering (there is little incentive to malinger in the survey situation), but because some illnesses may be incorrectly reported due to a lack of the relevant knowledge, and others, such as mental illness and venereal disease, may be under-reported since they have a social stigma.

The two indicators generally preferred are mortality rates and reported illness. Mortality rates are available for a wide variety of social groups; the statistics include information on the cause of death and are of high quality. Moreover, they do appear to correlate quite well with other data concerning ill-health, such as sickness benefit statistics and reported illness (Department of Health and Social Security, 1976, p. 16). Reported illness has the great advantage that it comes from the ultimate authority on peoples' aches and pains: the individuals themselves. Hence most of the available evidence concerns these two, a bias that is reflected in what follows.

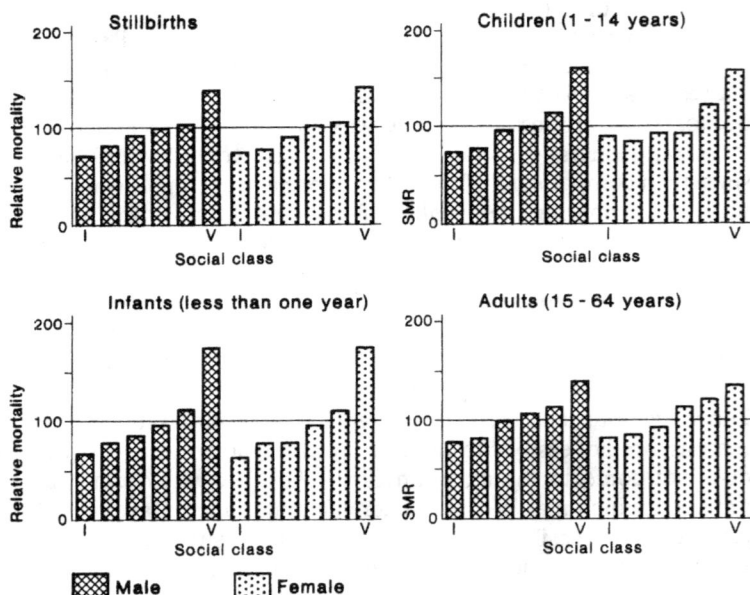

Figure 3.2 Mortality by social class. Relative mortality: ratio of rates for the social class to the rate for all males (females). SMR: standardised mortality ratio.

Source: Black (1980, p. 32). Originally published in OPCS, *Occupational Mortality 1970–72.*

To begin with mortality. Unfortunately there is no information available on the distribution of mortality between the main divisions of the population mentioned so far: socio-economic groups and income groups. But, as noted above, there is a substantial body of data concerning the distribution by social class. This has been usefully assembled in the Black Report; Figure 3.2 summarises its evidence for men and women at four different points in the life cycle. It is apparent that there is a substantial class gradient for both sexes at all points. (It should be noted that the relatively flatter gradient for adults than for infants and children is slightly misleading: a large difference for those in their twenties and thirties is offset by a steadily decreasing gap for those approaching pension age.) The significance of these differences will be appreciated if it is realised that they imply, *inter alia*:

- Children born into unskilled manual workers' families are four times more likely to die in their first year of life than those born into professional families.
- Boys aged between 1 and 14 in unskilled workers' families have twice the chance of death of boys in professional families; girls, over one-and-a-half times.
- Unskilled male workers are two-and-a-half-times as likely to die between the ages of 15 and 44 as professional workers.
- An individual born to professional parents, if he or she remains in that class, is likely to live over five years longer than one born into an unskilled manual household (Black, 1980, pp. 33–9).

Moreover, there is evidence to suggest that these differences may have become worse over time. Table 3.2 shows the standardised mortality ratios (a statistic, explained in a note,[11] which standardises mortality rates for differences in the age structures of the groups concerned) for adult males by social class for selected dates between 1930 and 1972. It is apparent that the gap between Social Classes I and V actually increased between 1930–32 and 1959–63, since when it has declined slightly. It is true that in these comparisons like is not being fully compared with like. The classifications changed somewhat over that time, and, even after this is taken into account, the proportion of the population in Social Class I has approximately doubled, and that in Social Class V dropped by a third, since 1930 (Black, 1980, p. 90, Table 3.16). But this does not allow us to dismiss the

Table 3.2   *Male Adult Mortality by Social Class, 1930–1972*

Men aged 15–65				*England and Wales*
Social class		*Standardised mortality ratios[a]*		
	1930–32	*1949–53*	*1959–63*	*1970–72*
I Professional	90	86	76	77
II Managerial	94	92	81	81
III Skilled manual and non-manual	97	101	100	104
IV Partly skilled	102	104	103	114
V Unskilled	111	118	143	137

[a] See note 11, p. 52.

Source: Black (1980), p. 65, Table 3.1.

phenomenon. The fact remains that the lowest groups in the population, even if they have shrunk somewhat in size, appear to be relatively as badly off in terms of health now as their equivalents were in the 1930s.

The distribution of reported illness has a similar pattern. Table 3.3 shows the percentage of each group that reported either acute sickness, chronic illness or both to the 1976 General Household Survey. To make them more comparable with the social class figures on mortality the top and the bottom SEGs have been split into two: the highest category (professionals) corresponds broadly to Social Class I and the lowest (unskilled manual workers) to Social Class V. The differences are manifest. Less than a fifth of those in families of professionals, employers and managers, reported themselves as ill in one way or another, compared with over a quarter of those from semi-skilled, and nearly a third of

Table 3.3   *Reported Illness by Socio-Economic Group*

All persons		*Great Britain, 1976*
Socio-economic group	*Percentage of group reporting illness[a]*	*Base (= 100 %)*
Professionals	17.0	1535
Employers and managers	18.7	4536
Intermediate and junior non-manual	22.9	6544
Skilled manual	21.9	11448
Semi-skilled manual	25.5	6053
Unskilled manual	32.1	1717

[a] Acute, chronic or both.

Source: General Household Survey, 1976, unpublished data.

those in unskilled, manual workers' families. These results are not a freak of the year concerned; the General Household Surveys from 1971 to 1975 all show similar patterns. Nor are they the result of differences in the age and sex composition of the various groups; age/sex standardisation of the 1972 figures showed some reduction in the inequality, but the basic pattern remained.[12]

Surveys of particular aspects of ill-health or particular groups show similar trends. Brown and Harris (1978) found that depression in inner cities showed this pattern of social class bias: 8 per cent of those in Social Classes I and II reported depression compared with 25 per cent in Classes IV and V. A recent survey of dental health found that the proportion of people with no natural teeth in Classes IV and V is substantially higher than that for the rest of the population (Royal Commission on the National Health Service, 1979, p. 107).

Such evidence as is available concerning the other two indicators of ill-health mentioned – medical records and days off sick – gives a similar picture. Data from medical records that do not suffer from the usual incomplete coverage problem are those derived from the medical examinations given in Scotland to all schoolchildren at the age of five. These show that, for instance, the proportion of children in Social Class V suffering from refractive error in eyesight was twice as great, and the proportion suffering from tooth decay over three times as great, as the proportion in Social Class I (Central Statistical Office, 1975, p. 27, Table 7.4). The General Household Survey for 1972 reported that those in the lowest socio-economic group had nearly six times more days off work due to sickness per person than those in the top group (OPCS, 1975, p. 207, Table 5.19).

So, whatever figures are chosen, they show inequalities in health to be a salient feature of British society. Moreover, they do not appear to have decreased significantly over time, and in particular, they do not seem to have diminished since the inception of the National Health Service.

Again this presents a puzzle. Why is it that, despite the provision of free medical care and despite all the advances in medical care of the last half century being made available to every one, inequalities in health remain as firmly entrenched as ever? One possible explanation is the inequality in medical care described in the previous section. If the middle class receive more medical attention per ill person, then it might be thought that we need look no further for the explanation of the inequalities in health itself; an explanation which has the obvious corollary that the appropriate policy is in some way to equalise the distribution of medical care. The Black Report, for instance, includes as part of its strategy for reducing inequalities in health various improvements in the NHS, including increased incentives for GPs to work in areas with a high prevalence of ill-health and improved systems of ante-natal and child care; recommendations that are presumably based in part on the belief that improvements in medical care for those lower down the social scale will significantly improve their health.

Unfortunately, beliefs of this kind are increasingly under attack. With the virtual elimination of most infectious diseases in developed countries, the major fatal diseases are now heart disease (which accounts for almost half of all deaths in Britain each year) and cancer. And, despite massive research efforts, there is little that medical science can do to cure either. The situation with many non-fatal illnesses is little better. Medical care can do little or nothing to cure rheumatism, arthritis, glaucoma and most respiratory diseases; the value of much obstetric technology is questionable; and some standard treatments for various illnesses have been shown to be quite ineffective and others actually harmful (for a useful summary, see Culyer, 1980, p. 211).

This apparent ineffectiveness of medical care (particularly for fatal diseases) is supported by statistical analysis of the determinants of mortality. Dennis Leech and Keith Cowling (1978) found that differences between areas in access to GPs (as measured by the number of patients per GP) bore no relation to differences in those areas' death rates, a finding confirmed by Forster (1979). A. L. Cochrane *et al.* (1978) in a study across several developed countries found the factors usually considered as indicators of the quality of medical care (including ratio of GPs to patients, numbers of acute hospital beds, etc.) have had no impact on reducing death rates of whatever kind (adult or infant). Indeed, it appeared that the greater the availability of doctors, the *higher* were the death rates.

Evidence such as this has led a noted American expert on health care, Victor Fuchs, to argue (1974, p. 6):

True advances in medical science, particularly the development of anti-infections drugs in the 1930's, 40's and 50's did much to reduce morbidity [ill-health] and mortality. Today, however, differences in health levels between the United States and other developed countries, or among populations in the United States are not related to differences in the quantity and quality of medical care.

Ivan Illich has gone further. He argues that the medical profession (and thus by implication the care it gives) is not only ineffective in promoting good health, but 'has become a major threat to health' (1976, p. 3). Existing forms of medical treatment induce further illness as often as they cure it. Moreover, they foster a socially unhealthy dependence of the population on the medical profession, and, through their emphasis on the preservation of life at all costs, deprive people of their ability to cope with suffering and death in a dignified fashion. Indeed he argues that the fact that the poor do not receive medical care proportional to their needs is actually a good thing; for 'more access, even though restricted to those who now receive less, would only equalise the delivery of professional illusions and torts' (p. 242).

Few would go as far as Illich. Some medical care is clearly effective. Examples are vaccination, some antibiotics, the control of diabetes and emergency surgery. Moreover, even that which is ineffective in curative terms often has an important role in alleviating discomfort and anxiety. To help reduce the physiological and psychological costs of a disease may be almost as important as curing the disease itself.

Nevertheless, the fact remains that death rates and general ill-health do not seem to be greatly affected by the availability of medical care. Interestingly, despite their recommendations for changes in the NHS, the authors of the Black Report appear implicitly to have accepted this view, for nowhere in their discussion of the determinants of inequality in health (1980, Ch. 6) are inequalities in medical care mentioned.

But if medical care is not an important determinant of people's health, then what is? A clue can be obtained from examining class gradients in the causes of mortality. The Black Report compared class gradients for different causes of death and found that the steepest gradients were, for infants, accidents and respiratory diseases; for children aged one to fourteen, again accidents, infective and parasitic diseases and pneumonia; for adults, infective and parasitic diseases, respiratory disease, diseases of the genito-urinary systems and, for males, accidents. The significant feature of almost all of these causes is that they are largely environmental in origin, a phenomenon which suggests that the socio-economic environment in which people live may be a crucial determinant of their states of health.

This hypothesis has received support in several statistical studies. Martini and his associates at the University of Nottingham (1977) found that composite socio-demographic indicators explained considerably more than indicators of medical care of variations across regions in infant mortality, total mortality, deaths in hospital and certified incapacity. Earlier research (such as Gardner, Crawford and Morris, 1969) had come to similar conclusions.

But these studies did not attempt to pinpoint precisely what features of the broad social and economic environment are the most important determinants of health. Possible candidates include occupation, housing conditions, air pollution and income levels. Studies which have included some or all of these variables separately have emerged with some interesting conclusions. Occupation, perhaps surprisingly, does not seem to be an important determinant of mortality on its own; for non-working and working members of households usually show the same pattern of mortality (Wilkinson, 1976b). Poor housing – although no doubt very important when infectious diseases were the major cause of ill-health – now does not seem greatly to affect general mortality (Wilkinson, 1976b; Forster, 1979), although Backett has suggested it may be an important determinant of accidents to children (1977, p. 104). Air pollution, on the other hand, does seem to make some contribution (Leech and Cowling, 1978, p. 25).

But the variable that often appears to be the most important is income (Wilkinson, 1976b; Leech and Cowling, 1978). Ill-health appears to be strongly related to low income. Why this should be is a matter of some dispute. Diet has always been considered to be an important determinant of health (see McKeown, 1976); and Wilkinson, in the study already mentioned, goes on to demonstrate this for his sample, and points out that the poor have diets that are noticeably inferior to those of the better off. The poor eat less fruit, less fresh green vegetables, less cheese, less milk and less meat than the rich; to make up for this, they eat more potatoes, more cereal products (mainly bread), and more sugar. Leech and Cowling agree that diet is important, but argue that there are a variety of other factors which are also income-related such as air pollution.

Alternatively, the relationship between ill-health and income (and indeed that between ill-health and social class) could be explained by reversing the link of causation. Rather than low levels of income creating ill-health, it could be argued that ill-health at least in part contributes to low levels of income. Those subject to chronic ill-health may find it more difficult to work, have to take on less demanding occupations (or give up work altogether) and hence drift to the bottom of the social scale. But, while this no doubt explains part of the correlation between ill-health and low social status, it is unlikely to be very significant; for, as we have seen, the inequalities in adult health are mirrored in the inequalities in children's health (which could not be explained by this hypothesis). Moreover, many manual occupations are very demanding physically, yet these occupations show an incidence of ill-health similar to the less demanding ones.

Another possible explanation for health inequalities concerns differences in the behaviour patterns of social groups. For instance, there are substantial differences between social groups in exercise and smoking – both now generally accepted as important determinants of health. In 1977, for example, the General Household Survey reported that over half of persons aged 16 and over in professional families engaged in some outdoor sport or activity compared with just 14 per cent in unskilled manual workers' families (OPCS, 1979, p. 125, Table 7.22). The 1976 Survey investigated smoking habits and found that those too varied substantially between SEGs: 58 per cent of unskilled men and 38 per cent of unskilled women were current smokers, compared with about a quarter of professional men and women (OPCS, 1978, p. 245, Table 8.33).

But simply to point to behaviour differences such as these is not quite sufficient as an explanation (or even as part of an explanation) of inequalities in health. For it begs the question concerning the source of those differences. They could be ascribed to differences in tastes or in the innate psychological make-up of individuals within each group; an explanation which some may find appealing, but for which there is no independent evidence. Alternatively, they could arise because of differences in the information available to the different groups, middle-class individuals, for instance, being arguably more aware of the dangers of smoking and lack of exercise than those in the working class. But the relative ineffectiveness of health education programmes in changing peoples' behaviour (to be discussed below) suggests that the simple presence or absence of the relevant information is not an important determinant of behaviour patterns.

A more plausible explanation for the differences concerns differences in the constraints that individuals face. In particular, differences in income levels may well be crucial. Nutritional food, such as fruit, is more expensive than its less desirable substitutes. Exercise can be costly, both in financial terms (many leisure activities require equipment) and in terms of time. Income differences can even create differences in tastes. Individuals brought up in poor households whose parents found it cheaper to buy white bread than brown, or to smoke a packet of cigarettes than to take a walk in the country, are likely to develop tastes that accord with their situations. Hence explanations for health inequalities in terms of behaviour differences are not necessarily alternatives for explanations that rely on differences in the socio-economic environment; rather, behaviour may be one of the routes through which the environmental influences work.

Richard Wilkinson, whose pioneering statistical work connecting mortality and income has already been mentioned, has reached similar conclusions, at least in so far as diet is concerned. Differences in dietary patterns, he argues, are more likely to be affected by differences in income than by differences in random tastes or in education because (Wilkinson, 1976a, p. 568):

First, statistical conditions *show* that diet is related more closely to income than education. Second, those people belonging to the middle and upper income groups who have large families to feed and clothe, tend to adopt dietary patterns more like smaller, lower income families. With additional children they may actually reduce their *total* family consumption of some expensive foodstuffs such as fruit. Third, while there is no significant difference between the number of calories consumed by high and low income groups, it is clear that the low income groups make up their total by buying more of the cheaper calories and less of the more expensive ones. The differences are not just chance differences in tastes (emphases in original).

As with inequalities in public expenditure, therefore, the principal explanation for the persistence of inequalities in health seems to be what the Black Report calls a 'materialist' or 'structural' one, that is, one which emphasises the role of economic and social factors. The report itself, after a careful review of all the evidence, comes to the conclusion that 'more of the relevant evidence' is explained by these factors 'than by any other form of explanation' (1980, p. 195). In short, as with inequalities in health care, inequalities in health reflect the wider inequalities in society.

Equality and Policy

The 1944 White Paper which announced the introduction of a comprehensive health service stated as its principal aim that 'everybody in the country ... should have an equal opportunity to benefit from ... medical and allied services' (*A National Health Service*, p. 47). More recently, the Working Party on the re-allocation of resources within the NHS gave as its principal objective the provision of 'equal opportunity of access to health care for people at equal risk' (Department of Health and Social Security, 1976, p. 7). The Royal Commission on the National Health Service included among a list of seven objectives two explicitly concerned with equality: 'equality of entitlement to health services ... without respect to age, social class, sex, race or religion' and 'equality of access to these services' (1979, p. 9). Dr David Owen, one time Minister of State for Health, described the 'central task of the National Health Service' as the 'ultimate abolition of the present inequalities in health provision and care' (1976, p. 60), a task to which his successor, David Ennals, added the objective of narrowing 'the gap in health standards between different social classes' (Black, 1980, p. 1).

Equality of some kind is thus a major aim of policy makers concerned with the National Health Service. Following the review of the evidence concerning distribution in the earlier sections of this chapter, we are now in a position to assess the extent to which this aim has been achieved. To do so properly, however, it is necessary to be more specific about the kinds of equality that are of concern; and it is with this that we begin.

Objectives

Of the possible interpretations of equality discussed in Chapter 2, those which appear to conform most closely to policy makers' (and others') egalitarian aims concerning the NHS are *equality of use*, *equality of cost* and *equality of outcome*. The White Paper's objective, the Royal Commission's first objective and David Owen's statement can best be interpreted as expressing the aim of equal treatment for equal need, a goal which, as was noted in Chapter 2, is a specific version of the equality of use objective. In other words, all those in the group labelled 'equal need' should consume health care equally, regardless of income, occupation or social status. The objective of the Resource Allocation Working Party and the second Royal Commission objective can be taken to refer to equality of cost; for, if the private cost to an individual of obtaining health treatment varies with his or her social and economic circumstances, then it seems reasonable to suppose that neither 'equality of access' nor 'equality of opportunity of access' has been achieved. Finally, David Ennals' statement clearly refers to equality of the 'outcome' of the NHS, that is, health itself.

Reality

Whichever of these interpretations is chosen, it seems not to have been realised. Equality of use for equality of need has not been achieved, if need is defined as self-reported illness. The evidence suggests that the top socio-economic group receives 40 per cent more NHS expenditure per person reporting illness than the bottom one. Moreover, this almost certainly underestimates the overall inequality in the consumption of medical care, partly because of biases in the method of calculation and partly because the estimates ignore care that is privately financed.

Equality of cost (and hence of access) has not been achieved. There still exist substantial differences in the expenditure of time that different social groups have to make if they wish to use the service. Those lower down the social scale have to travel further, by slower means of transport, and have to wait longer having once arrived. Nor are the differences simply those of time; unlike many middle-class users of the NHS, most working-class users lose income if they have to take time off from work, money they can often ill afford to lose.

Inequalities of outcome also persist. Compared with the children in professional families, those in unskilled manual workers' families are four times more likely to die in their first year of life, and about twice as likely to die in the next forty years. Overall, individuals born to professional parents will live between 5 and 10 per cent longer than those from unskilled households. The statistics of reported illness in recent years show the same pattern, with proportionately nearly twice as many unskilled manual workers and their families reporting illness as professionals.

However, there is one possible interpretation of equality that does come close to being achieved: that of equality of public expenditure per person (ill and not ill) between social groups, regardless of need. Such a conclusion is not of great relevance to the objectives of the NHS, at least as put forward in official statements, but it could be important for any assessment of the overall distributional impact of public expenditure.

The NHS has thus failed to achieve full equality, except perhaps in the limited sense of equality of public expenditure between SEGs regardless of need. But has it at least achieved greater equality? Is there, as a result of the operations of the National Health Service, more equality in public expenditure, use, costs, outcomes or final incomes? Here the answers must be more tentative, partly because of the difficulties discussed in Chapter 2 of choosing a standard of comparison and partly because of the absence of the relevant data. If the standard is the distribution that prevailed prior to the introduction of the NHS, then, although there is little earlier information, some guesses can be made. As Abel-Smith (1958) has noted, the institution of the NHS made a service free to the middle class that previously was only free to the working class; in doing so, it may have created greater equality in money costs and in public expenditure, although in a direction that an egalitarian might find perverse. The effects on differences in use are harder to predict. The abolition of means tests and general improvements in quality almost certainly increased working-class use, but the reduction in costs for the middle classes will have increased their use as well. Finally, in the one area where there are data – outcomes as measured by mortality rates – inequality has actually increased. The gap between the classes' mortality rates was narrower in 1930–32 than it was in 1970–72.

Prospects for Policy

What are the implications of this for policy? Does the apparent failure of public expenditure in health care to achieve equality imply that such expenditure should be drastically reduced, or even eliminated? Should the NHS be abolished, and the allocation of medical care be returned to the market? Or are there less dramatic changes which could improve the system's ability to achieve greater equality, while at the same time preserving its essential character?

The effect on equality of abolishing the NHS would depend crucially upon what was done with the public funds that were saved thereby. If these were used to increase the cash incomes of the poor, then it is likely that greater equality, in at least some of the senses of the term, would be achieved. There would be greater equality in final income, since, if everything else remained the same (an important qualification) an element of that income which appears to be broadly equally distributed per head would be replaced by one which is pro-poor. If the evidence suggesting that health is heavily dependent on income is correct, then reducing inequality in the latter will reduce inequality in the former. It is even possible that there would be fewer inequalities in use relative to need. Both rich and poor would face the same increase in the cost of medical care, but the poor would have (relatively) higher incomes with which to meet those costs.

Of course, there is no guarantee that if the NHS were abolished, the savings to the public budget would be used in this way. It is perhaps just as likely that they would be distributed equally or perhaps used to raise the incomes of the rich (through, say, cuts in the higher rates of income tax). In either case, none of the above conclusions would hold; indeed they might even be reversed. Moreover, there are numerous reasons, quite unconnected with the question of equality, why the NHS should not be replaced by the private market. Market allocation of a commodity will be socially inefficient if the commodity has 'external benefits'[13] or substantial consumer ignorance associated with it, and medical care has both. There are monopolistic elements in, among other things, the supply of medical practitioners and of drugs. The NHS, being itself a (virtual) monopoly purchaser of these factors, can play an important role in keeping down their costs.[14] More generally, it has been argued (notably by Titmuss, 1970) that non-market allocation systems increase the opportunities for altruistic behaviour and hence encourage a wider diffusion of that behaviour, a desirable end in itself.

All in all, therefore, it does not seem as though the appropriate conclusion to be drawn from the evidence reviewed earlier in the chapter is that the NHS should be abolished. But, if it is to be preserved, is it possible to reduce the inequalities documented? In particular, is it possible to reform the system so as to significantly affect inequalities in the areas of most social concern: costs, outcomes and use relative to need?

The explanation for inequality in use relative to need put forward in the previous section suggests that there may be three different ways in which greater equality could be achieved:

- Policies designed to change suppliers' behaviour. An example would be changes in staff training so as to increase general awareness within the NHS of the difficulties faced by, and to improve the ability of medical personnel to communicate with, working-class patients. Also, a change in NHS recruitment policies might be in order, so as to favour those from working-class origins.
- Policies to alter working-class perceptions of the benefits from NHS health care. These perceptions are affected by suppliers' behaviour, and therefore any policies designed to alter these should have some effect here too. Also, general improvements in health education, as recommended by, for example, Morris (1979) and the Black Report (1980), could increase working-class perceptions of the benefits from health care, particularly those from preventive measures.
- Policies designed to raise middle-class costs relative to working-class costs. An example would be the relocation of medical facilities away from middle-class areas to working-class ones, coupled with financial inducements to medical practitioners to move (again as recommended in the Black Report); another is the extension of means-tested charges, often recommended by conservative bodies of various kinds.

In practice, however, it is difficult to see the first two of these having more than a marginal impact. Changes in hospital staff training seem unlikely to have a great effect; class attitudes are well-entrenched by the time most training is undertaken. Recruitment of working-class staff may have the opposite effect to that intended, since those who have succeeded in 'escaping' their working-class origins are often the least sympathetic to those who have not (as illustrated by the following story: When the results of the study of the distribution of public expenditure on health care were released, I suggested in a radio interview a change in recruitment policy along the lines described. A few days later, I received an angry letter from a doctor of working-class origins. In it he claimed that the people who really abused the NHS were his 'old buddies from way back': average working-class men 'out for a bit of crafty manipulation of the welfare system'. The truly ill, on the other hand, were 'non-manual workers suffering from the effects of responsibility', and they got the 'proper time given to them'.). Nor would it be wise to place too much hope on health education programmes, for those which have been tried are noted for their ineffectiveness (Gatherer *et al.*, 1979).

There is perhaps more scope for policies designed to change relative costs. Following the report of the Resource Allocation Working Party, serious attempts are being made to reallocate resources to those regions which have a higher proportion of low income households. The extension of means-tested charges would raise the cost to the high income groups, hence perhaps reducing their use relative to that of low income groups, while at the same time perhaps promoting greater equality of cost.

But again it is far from clear that these changes would make a very significant impact. Regional reallocations will not affect class differences within regions, as pointed out by Bosanquet in an excellent critique of the reallocation procedures (1980a); and the outcome of government attempts to relocate industry and its own departments suggests that it is not easy to persuade high income professionals to live and work in deprived areas or regions, even with very substantial financial inducements. Similarly, experience with means-tested schemes is not encouraging. Their extension throughout the NHS would require patients to fill out substantial forms, taking up time and effort, the more so for those unpractised in writing skills. The truth of the information on the forms would have to be checked, necessitating the threat of humiliating enquiries, and in some cases the reality of them. Even when this process is complete, the eventual receipt of the free service, for which others are paying, may in itself be humiliating. Hence both the time and psychological cost of using the service would be increased, even to those who had to pay no charge. The likely result would be to discourage both middle- and working-class use of the NHS, an outcome which many would view as undesirable in itself, and which, in any case, would have little impact on relative inequality.

In fact it is difficult to resist the conclusion that there is little the Health Service can do to reduce inequality in its use or in the private cost of that use. The principal determinants are largely beyond its control. Rather, they stem from basic social and economic inequalities, that is, the inequalities in income which lead to inequalities in car and telephone ownership; the differences in working conditions that leave some individuals free to attend the doctor without losing money, but others not; the class divisions that render different groups in society mistrustful of, and hostile to, each other. Inequality in health care reflects inequality in society. It seems that one cannot be altered without affecting the other.

The prospects for reforming the Health Service so as to promote greater equality in health itself seem little better. If it is indeed the case that much medical care is largely ineffective then, even if it were possible to increase use of the Health Service's facilities by the poor relative to the rich, this would have little effect on outcomes. Rather, the evidence suggests that, as with inequalities in health care, the best way to reduce inequalities in health significantly is to reduce inequalities in income, and that is beyond the scope of policies concerned with the delivery of health care alone.

Overall, therefore, it does not appear there is very much further that can be done within the scope of the NHS to reduce inequalities in health or health care. As noted earlier, this does not imply that the NHS should be abolished or even curtailed; it has many achievements to its credit. But what does appear to follow from the discussion is that too much should not be expected from the free provision of medical care with respect to inequality. The scope for using the NHS as a tool for eliminating inequalities in health or health care is limited, for they reflect the basic structure of social and economic inequality.

Notes to Chapter 3

1 Appendix B, Table B.1.

2 For non-technical expositions of the relevant arguments, see Le Grand and Robinson (1976, Ch. 2), Abel-Smith (1976, Chs 3 and 4) or Culyer (1976, Ch. 7).

3 Other writers who have discussed the problem include Townsend (1974), the contributors to Carter and Peel (1976) and Morris (1979). A comprehensive review of the evidence is available in the recently published Black Report (1980).

4 There have been several studies of the overall distribution of taxes and public expenditure in Britain by income group (listed in Appendix A, p. 155). However, these generally allocated public expenditure on the social services, including health care, to different income groups on the basis of simple *a priori* assumptions (e.g. equal expenditure per head). The distribution of public expenditure on health care is also included in the annual studies of the incidence of taxes and benefits produced by the Central Statistical Office; for an example, see Appendix B, Table B.3. However, again these are not based on data concerning the actual use by different groups; instead, each individual of the same age and sex is simply assumed to make the same use of the Health Service. Townsend (1979, pp. 218–23) does include health care in his study of the aggregate value of public social services to different income groups, a study which is based on use as revealed in a large sample survey. Unfortunately, the health care estimates are not published separately.

5 It was thus assumed that the 'nominal' beneficiaries (actual users) were the actual beneficiaries. For further discussion of the implications of this assumption, and of the omission of capital expenditure, see Appendix A.

6 OPCS (1979, pp. 91–3, Tables 6.23, 6.26 and 6.30). See also OPCS (1980, p. 122, Table 7.9).

7 Personal communication.

8 See Figure 6.2.

9 OPCS (1978, p. 148, Table 5.36).

10 The occupational classification used was that of the National Readership Survey. The term middle class referred to the classifications A, B and C1, corresponding broadly to the Registrar General's Social Classes I, II and IIIN; the term working class referred to the remainder.

11 The standardised mortality ratio is calculated by estimating the deaths that would have been expected in the group concerned if the death rates for that group at each age had been the same as the average for the population as a whole, and then expressing these as a ratio to actual deaths × 100. Thus an SMR of 80, for instance, implies that actual deaths in the group were 80 per cent of those which would have been expected if each of the group's members of a particular age had exactly the same chance of dying at that age as the average for the population.

12 Both the actual and age/sex standardised figures for 1972 are given in Le Grand (1978, p. 129, Table I, Cols (5) and (6)). The age/sex standardisation was actually undertaken by Forster (1976). Regrettably, there is an error in

Col. (5) of that table, the estimate for SEG 1 being transposed from another column; it should read 12.0, not 9.5.

13   For the definition of external benefits, see Appendix A, pp. 162. For the development of this and of the other arguments for the inefficiency of market allocation of medical care, see the references listed in note 2.

14   The NHS purchases drugs at well below international levels (Cooper and Cooper, 1972). In the UK in the mid 1970s doctors earned less than three times the average male industrial earnings, compared with six times in the USA and in West Germany, and seven times in France (Office of Health Economics, 1979, p. 12).

CHAPTER 4

Education

> Education, then, beyond all other devices of human origin,
> is the great equalizer of the conditions of men – the balance
> wheel of social machinery. *Horace Mann*

> To find a strategy for educational roads to equality! That has
> been a central theme of educational discussion from the
> beginning of the twentieth century. *A. H. Halsey*

Public spending dominates the educational systems of all
contemporary societies. In Britain, the state provides nursery,
primary and secondary schools, special schools for the
handicapped, evening institutes for adult education and leisure
classes, technical colleges, polytechnics and universities – all
largely free of direct charges or at heavily subsidised prices.
Education spending is the second largest item of government
expenditure (after social security); in 1978–9 it amounted to
nearly £9,000 million, 13 per cent of total public expenditure in
Great Britain.[1]

State involvement in education has been justified in a number
of ways. These include the necessity to stimulate economic
growth, to advance culture and to promote social cohesion and
national unity. But perhaps the major motivation has been the
pursuit of equality, a theme that has appeared in the writings and
public pronouncements of innumerable social thinkers and policy
makers. Hence it is important to establish the actual distributional
impact of education policies as far as possible; and that is the task
of the first two sections of this chapter. The first section examines
recent evidence concerning the distribution of public expenditure
on education in Britain, and offers some possible explanations for
that distribution. The second considers evidence concerning the
distribution of what are often considered to be the 'outcomes' of

educational policy – in particular, educational qualifications, social mobility and earnings – and discusses briefly the relationship of these distributions to education. Finally, the third section, 'Equality and Policy', specifies in as precise a form as possible the various egalitarian objectives that have at one time or another influenced educational policy, compares them with the actual distributions revealed in the previous two sections, and discusses the prospects for reform.

The Distribution of Public Expenditure

A breakdown of direct public expenditure on education by type of education in 1978–9 is given in Figure 4.1. In that year the largest consumers of public funds were secondary schools, taking up about a third of total capital and current expenditure on education.[2] Primary schools were the next largest, with over a fifth of current expenditure and about a quarter of capital expenditure. Further education and universities together took about a third of both capital and current expenditure (including student awards), with about half of that going to universities. Education for the under fives received 3 per cent of capital, and 2 per cent of current expenditure; school meals, milk and miscellaneous services took up approximately 11 per cent of current expenditure.

One item of public expenditure, small in amount but politically controversial, is not included in Figure 4.1. That is 'tax expenditures' for independent schools, which are the reductions in government revenue due to various tax reliefs to which the schools are entitled compared with the revenue which would have been obtained if the tax reliefs did not exist. Rogers (1980) has usefully summarised the relevant information. Independent schools are eligible for charitable status; they therefore gain partial exemption from rates and are also exempted from income tax on their profits, capital gains tax and capital transfer tax. Further, parents can get tax relief on any life endowment policies they use to fund their children's education. The total cost of the rate relief is small (estimated at £1 million in 1978), but that of the income tax provisions rather larger (£35 million).[3]

Estimates of the distribution of public expenditure on education have been produced annually for income groups by the

CURRENT

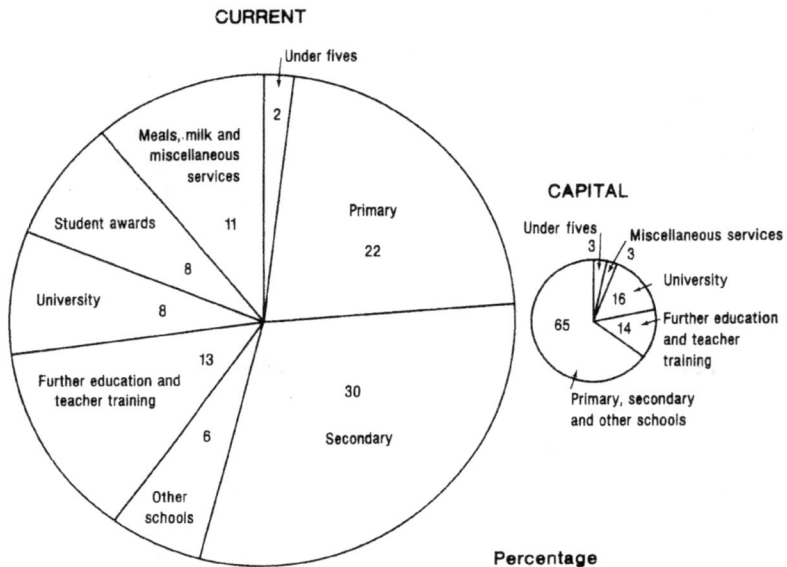

Figure 4.1 Public expenditure on education by category, Great Britain 1978–9.

Source: Appendix B, Table B.2.

Central Statistical Office (CSO) and for socio-economic groups (SEGs) in 1973 by the present author. Both assume that the only beneficiaries of the public education system are those currently using it, and both ignore capital expenditure (for discussion of the implications of those assumptions, see Appendix A).

The CSO estimates are based on the Family Expenditure Survey (FES).[4] Households are grouped according to the information they supply to the FES concerning their 'original' income, that is, income before taxation or receipt of any cash payments, such as social security, or of any other benefits from the state. The number of persons in each group using each sector of the public education system is obtained from the FES; these numbers are then multiplied by the annual current cost per pupil/ student for each sector, as estimated by the Department of Education and Science.[5] This gives the cost of the use of each sector's resources by each income group. For households containing students in receipt of maintenance awards, the actual value of those awards is added to the figures, and the fees and contributions made by parents subtracted. Adding the resultant numbers across all sectors gives the total cost of public education for each income group.

The estimates for 1978 are illustrated in Figure 4.2; the actual numbers are given in Appendix B, Table B.3. They show a distribution that is markedly pro-rich. On average, households in the richest fifth of the original income distribution received nearly one-and-a-half times as much public expenditure on education as the mean, and nearly three times as much as households in the poorest fifth. However, this impression of stark inequality is slightly misleading, for it arises at least in part from differences in the age structure and size of the relevant households. In particular, many of the very poor are elderly and hence would not be expected to make much use of the education system. Also, the poorer households tend to be smaller; if the distribution were calculated on a per person basis rather than a per household one, the distribution would be less unequal.[6]

The SEG estimates are discussed in detail in Le Grand (1980). The method of calculation may be summarised as follows. Data were available from the 1973 GHS on the numbers of persons in each sector of public education, broken down according to the SEG of their father (or head of household where the father was

All Households   United Kingdom, 1978

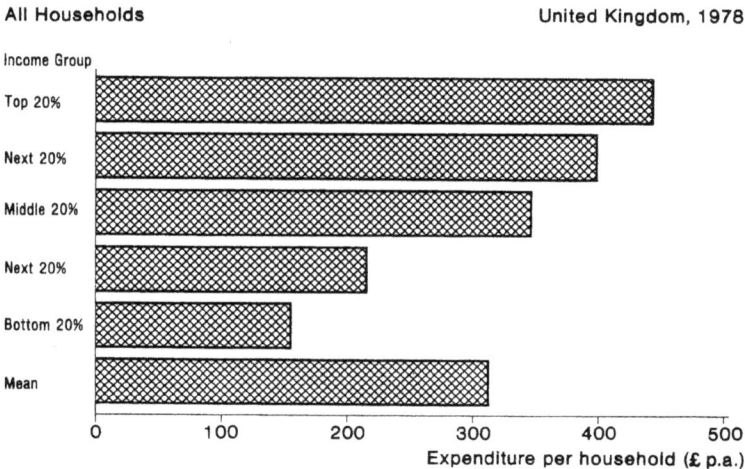

Figure 4.2   Public expenditure on education by income group.
Source: Appendix B, Table B.3.

absent). In a similar fashion to the CSO studies, these were multiplied by the cost per pupil/student for each sector to obtain the total public expenditure of the resources in each sector used by each SEG. These were then divided by the number of persons in the SEG's 'client population' for that sector of education, the client population being defined as the age range from which that sector drew its pupils/students. This gave the expenditure per person in the client population for each SEG.

Some of the results are shown in Table 4.1. The last column of the table shows that, when all the different sectors of education are taken together, the top SEG received over one-and-a-quarter times the mean public expenditure and about one-and-a-half times as much as the lowest SEG. This arose because, although people in the top SEG received slightly less state expenditure on primary and secondary education for pupils under 16 (presumably because they made a greater use of private education), they received substantially more expenditure in all the other sectors. For secondary pupils over 16 they received over

Table 4.1   *Public Expenditure on Education by Socio-Economic Group*

All persons					*England and Wales 1973*	
Socio-economic group	*Expenditure per person in client population[a] : percentage of mean*					
	Primary	*Secondary, pupils under 16*	*Secondary, pupils over 16*	*Further education*	*University*	*Total[b]*
Professional, employers and managers	90	88	165	149	272	128
Intermediate and junior non-manual	102	99	134	133	172	121
Skilled manual	103	105	65	99	37	89
Semi- and unskilled manual	103	103	91	43	50	84
Mean (£) = 100	139.7	206.0	65.3	17.2	16.3	70.7

[a] Client population: population in age range whence sector draws most of its pupils/students.

[b] Includes nursery education and evening institutes.

Source: Le Grand (1980, p. 7, Table I).

one-and-a-half times the mean and nearly twice that for the lowest SEG; for further education, one-and-a-half times the mean and three-and-a-half times that of the lowest; and for universities, nearly two-and-three-quarter times the mean, and over *five times* that of the lowest.

These estimates do not suffer from the same problems as the estimates by income group, at least not to the same extent. They are presented on a per person basis, so they are not affected by differences in household size. There are differences in the age and sex structure between SEGs, but they are not nearly as pronounced as those between income groups. Moreover, when the results were standardised for age and sex differences, the overall pattern remained largely unaltered (Le Grand, 1980, p. 7, Table I).

There are two other problems, however. First, because the relevant data were not available from the GHS, these results do not include maintenance awards for students. A crude attempt was made to adjust for this; it yielded a slight lessening of the inequality for further and university education (Le Grand, 1980, p. 8 and note 1). Also, the estimates assumed that costs per pupil were constant within each sector, an assumption that was unlikely to be fulfilled in the secondary sector in particular in 1973, due to the smaller degree of comprehensivisation. Since it is likely that the cost per pupil at establishments with a greater proportion of the higher SEGs was higher (such as grammar schools with superior teacher/pupil ratios), this implies that the results may underestimate the true inequality.

Two items of public expenditure on education have not yet been considered: school meals and tax expenditures to independent schools. Bleddyn Davies (1968) investigated the distribution of the school meals subsidy in 1965 and 1966. This subsidy had two components: one (about 20 per cent of the total) being the subsidy to free meals recipients, the other (the remaining 80 per cent) being the subsidy to children who took meals and paid for them. On the basis of FES data concerning the private expenditure by households on school meals he concluded that, while the first component of the subsidy, being means-tested, benefited the less well off, the second had the reverse effect: 'the higher the household income, the greater the school meals subsidy enjoyed' (p. 52). There have been no studies of the distributional effects of the tax expenditures for independent schools, but there can be little doubt that these also accrue largely to the better off.

Overall, therefore, it seems that, while public expenditure on compulsory education slightly favours the lower social groups, expenditure on the post-compulsory sectors strongly favours the better off – with the possible exception of student awards. Evidence from other countries show a similar pattern. In France, the 'liberal professions' are notably over-represented at universities and Instituts Universitaire de Technologie, compared with their proportion in the population, while agricultural and industrial workers are significantly under-represented (Neave, 1976, p. 79, Table 7.2). Fields (1975) investigated the distribution of the Kenyan higher education system and concluded that, as for Britain, 'the children of the relatively well-to-do benefit more from Kenya's higher education system than the children of poorer families and that this tendency is most pronounced at the University level' (p. 245). Selowsky's study of public subsidies to education in Colombia found that, while the distribution of public primary and secondary education was markedly pro-poor (due to the existence of a strong private sector patronised by the better off), public higher education favoured the better off. Indeed it did so to such an extent that it more than offset the pro-poor subsidy to the other sectors; the aggregate subsidy per capita for public education as a whole was about 75 per cent larger for households in the richest fifth of the population than for those in the poorest (1979, pp. 63–8). Meerman calculated the distribution of public expenditure (including, notably, capital expenditure) per person of school age in Malaysia; again the distribution favoured the rich (1979, pp. 128–9). Pechman (1970), reworking data from Hansen and Weisbrod's study of subsidies to higher education in California (1969), found that in 1965 these subsidies systematically benefited the higher income groups.[7] Windham (1970) found similar results for public higher education in Florida.

What of changes over time? The distribution of public expenditure reflects the distribution of use of the public education system; and, although there are no substantive estimates of the former prior to the 1960s,[8] there is some evidence concerning the latter. The Robbins Report on Higher Education produced evidence showing that the relative proportions of boys from manual and non-manual occupational classes entering university changed little between 1928–47 and 1960 (*Higher Education, Appendix I, p. 54*). However, these figures do not allow for changes in the class composition of the population as a whole over that time. Evidence which does not suffer from this problem, but which none the less tells the same story, comes from the work of Professor A. H. Halsey and his associates at Nuffield College, Oxford (Halsey, Heath and Ridge, 1980). This was based on the Oxford Social Mobility Project and used a survey of 8,500 men, aged between 20 and 60, undertaken in the early summer of 1972. The men were divided into age groups, or 'cohorts', according to their year of birth. The first cohort, for instance, included all those in the sample who were born between 1913 and 1922, while the last covered all those born between 1943 and 1952. Each cohort was further divided into a 'service' class, an 'intermediate' class and a 'working' class, classifications that very broadly correspond to the GHS classifications of professionals, employers and managers; intermediate and junior non-manual; and skilled, semi- and unskilled manual workers. The service class comprised about 14 per cent of their total sample, the intermediate class 31 per cent, and the working class 55 per cent.

Some of the results are summarised in Table 4.2. The first column shows the proportion of each class who went to university in the first and last cohorts. Although the proportions had increased for all three classes, the smallest increases, both absolutely and relatively, accrued to the working class. The second column of the table shows the average age at which the

Table 4.2 *Post-Compulsory Education by Occupational Class: Changes Over Time*

Males				*England and Wales*
Occupational class of father	*Percentage of each class attending university*		*Average age on taking up first job*	
	1913–22 cohort	*1943–52 cohort*	*1913–22 cohort*	*1943–47[a] cohort*
Service class	7	26	16.8	18.1
Intermediate class	2	8	15.0	16.2
Working class	1	3	14.4	15.6
All	2	9	n.a.[b]	n.a.[b]

[a] Figures include only those aged 25 or over in 1972.
[b] Not available in source tables.
Source: Halsey *et al.* (1980, p. 188, Table 10.8; p. 207, Table 11.2).

first job was taken up, and hence at which full-time education stopped. Again this shows a (slight) increase of the absolute gap between the classes. The researchers concluded that their results illustrated a 'sad story', viz.: 'the class differences were the same in the 1960s as they had been in the 1920s, despite a relatively favourable demography, economic growth and rising educational investment' (p. 207).

As with health care, the evidence concerning the distribution of public expenditure on education presents something of a puzzle. Why is it that, despite the availability of education from nursery school to university to everyone at no charge, the lower social groups receive so much less public expenditure than those from higher groups? Why is it that class differences in use do not seem to have even diminished significantly over the last fifty years, despite an enormous increase in state involvement and subsidisation?

The answers to these questions lie in the differences in the choices made by all the people involved. The latter can be divided into three groups: the child, the family (particularly the parents) and the education 'suppliers' (those who control the admissions procedures for educational institutions). All of these are affected by factors which operate differently for working-class children than for those of the middle class. Let us examine the process of choice in more detail.[9]

First, the child's decision, and for this, as with health care, it is helpful to use a simple model of rational behaviour. Individuals, in making the decision whether or not to demand an extra 'unit' of education (such as staying on an extra year at school or at college), will assess the perceived benefits and costs to them of that unit. If the former outweigh the latter, they will demand it; if not, they will not. The perceived benefits are of two kinds: 'consumption' and 'investment'. The consumption benefits are those which individuals receive while they are actually being educated, that is, the pleasures of learning, the extra-curricular opportunities for sports or cultural activities and so on. The investment benefits are those which individuals receive after the education unit is completed. These include any increase in income over and above that which they would otherwise have received; they may also include the richer and more meaningful life which many believe education makes possible.

The costs to individuals are the satisfactions they forgo while pursuing their education. These will depend on their perceptions of how much they could have earned had they not been in education (net of any extra they might have to contribute to household expenses), the proportion of the direct costs of their education (purchase of books, etc.) which they have to bear, and the loss of the extra freedom which they may associate with working life.

Now both benefits and costs are likely to differ between social groups. Working-class children, brought up by parents with little education themselves, are unlikely to value highly the consumption benefits from education. Also, again due to a lack of parental experience, they will have less information than middle-class children of the investment benefits of education, particularly with respect to any increases in income which they can expect to receive; hence they may perceive the investment as worth less, and more risky, than it actually is. So the perceived benefits for working-class children are likely to be smaller than those for the children of middle-class families.[10]

The costs, on the other hand, will almost certainly be greater for people from working-class families. This is not necessarily because the cost in terms of money will be greater; the direct costs of purchasing books and so on will be similar for all children, and the costs in terms of the size of forgone earnings may actually be lower for working-class than for middle-class children, since they would have fewer job opportunities without education. But it is not the cost in terms of money that is relevant to the decision; rather, it is the cost in terms of the satisfaction or pleasure forgone. Since it is reasonable to assume that each pound forgone represents a greater sacrifice for those from low income than those from high income families, the same (or even smaller) money costs for the former are likely to be a more important barrier to education than for the latter.

The parents' decisions will be affected by many of the same factors as the children's. In particular, as far as benefits are concerned, working-class parents may be just as sceptical, if not more so, than their children. More importantly, they may fear the effect of education on the child's attitudes and loyalties; they may be afraid of the 'loss' of their child.

Parental costs will also differ across the classes. David Piachaud (1975) has attempted to estimate the differences in these costs between a child continuing education and going to work. The additional costs of a child continuing education he specified as the extra cost of maintenance (food, clothes, pocket money, etc.), minus any tax allowances, child benefit or student grant received, plus the forgone contribution to family income which the child would have made, had he or she been working. He found that, primarily because of the means-tested student grant, the money costs of keeping a child aged between 18 and 20 in full-time education for high income parents (those earning twice average male earnings in manufacturing industry) was considerably greater than for low income parents (two-thirds of male manufacturing earnings). But at the more crucial age of 15 to 17, the cost differences were reversed, with the low income parents paying more in absolute terms than those with high incomes, a gap that is even more dramatic if considered in terms of forgone satisfactions rather than money.

So, for both children and parents, the benefits of continuing education are likely to be greater, and the costs less, for the middle class than the working class. What of the influence of 'suppliers'? If none of the benefit/cost considerations were relevant, and the demands for continued education were the same for all classes, would we then expect equality of use? It is unlikely. For most institutions of continuing education require potential entrants to meet certain admission criteria, particularly the passing of exams. And, as will be seen in the next section, examination results are quite unevenly distributed between the classes.

Finally, there is one explanation not yet considered. Some believe that the working class are unable to 'defer their gratification' to the same extent as the middle class. In this view, working-class individuals are less capable than their middle-class counterparts of imagining the future, and hence of undertaking sacrifices now in order to obtain rewards later. This psychological incapacity means that they are not prepared to make the financial and other sacrifices necessary to continue their education beyond the school-leaving age, even though such sacrifices would bring them considerable long-term rewards.[11]

Now it cannot be too strongly emphasised that there is no independent evidence to support this alleged incapacity of the working class to foresee the future. Often, the evidence that is cited is precisely the phenomenon which it is trying to explain: differences between working- and middle-class demand for education. As has been shown there are plenty of other possible explanations for the phenomenon, explanations that can be verified independently, and which do not rely on dubious interpersonal judgements about psychological capabilities. Hence, in the absence of independent evidence, this explanation has to be rejected.

The Distribution of Educational Outcomes

Suitable measures of the outcome of education are not easily available. Indicators of performance such as educational qualifications are suspect because they measure a limited aspect of educational achievement, and because they do not capture the broader impact of education on society. Measures which do attempt to encompass the latter, such as earnings differences or indicators of occupational mobility, have been challenged on the grounds that they are little affected by education. It is impossible in the space available here to resolve all the relevant issues. Instead, a summary of some of the evidence available concerning the distribution of the indicators mentioned – educational qualifications, occupational mobility and earnings – is presented, together with a brief discussion of the role of education in determining those distributions. Regrettably, much of the evidence quoted refers to men; that for women is either not available or more complex to interpret.

Educational Qualifications

There is no published information on the distribution of educational qualifications by parental income group. But the work of Halsey and others on the Oxford Social Mobility Project provides information concerning the distribution of (males') educational qualifications by occupational class of their fathers. This is summarised in Figure 4.3, whence it is apparent that there existed substantial inequalities between the three classes. Over half of those with fathers in the service class obtained at least one O-level or equivalent, and over a quarter one A-level or equivalent, compared with 12 and 7 per cent respectively for the working class. If attendance at university can be taken as a good indicator of obtaining a university degree, then it appears that a fifth of sons with service-class fathers obtained a degree, compared with only 5 per cent of sons with working-class fathers.

Men   **England and Wales**

Occupational class
of father:

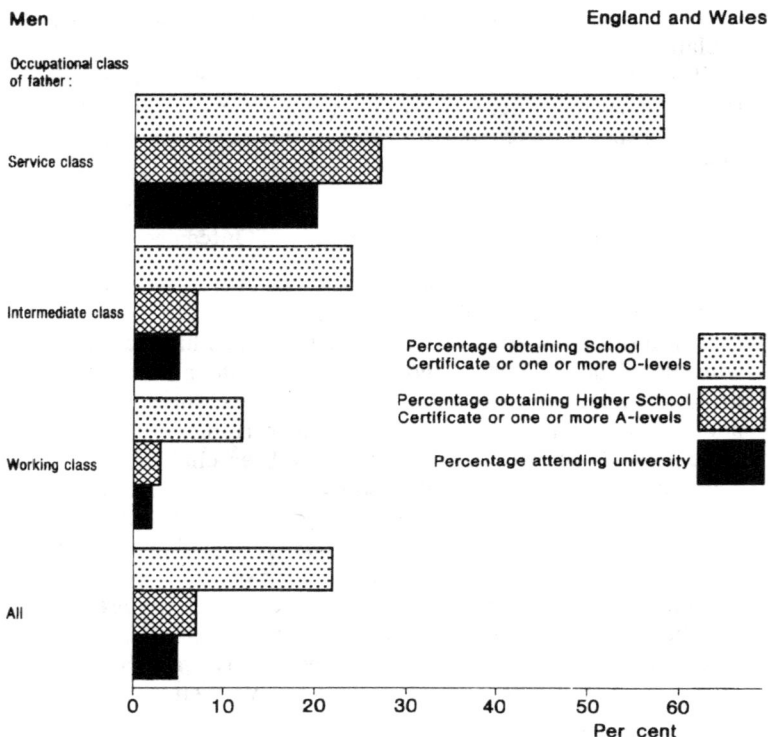

Figure 4.3   Educational qualifications by occupational class.
Source: Halsey *et al.* (1980, p. 184, Table 10.5).

There is also a range of earlier evidence concerning the distribution by occupational class not only of educational
qualifications, but also of educational skills. This is usefully summarised in Reid (1977, pp. 173–91). Among others there are
studies showing that:

- 7-year-old children from Social Class V are six times more
  likely to be poor readers, and over three times more likely to
  be poor at arithmetic, than Social Class I children;
- over 90 per cent of professional and managerial children at
  maintained grammar schools with eleven-plus scores in the
  top third gained five or more O-level passes, compared with

under half of those from the families of semi- and unskilled manual workers;

- in the top sixth of the ability range, as measured by intelligence tests at 15, the percentage of children whose parents and grandparents were in non-manual occupations, and who gained at least four O-level passes, was more than twice that of children whose parents and grandparents were in manual occupations.

Overall, it is apparent that whatever other results public expenditure in education may have achieved, it has not succeeded in equalising the educational qualifications of children from different social backgrounds, even for those with similar abilities.

Part of the explanation for these differences doubtless lies in the fact there is inequality in the consumption of education itself. This is of two kinds: inequality within the public sector described earlier in the chapter, and inequality between the public and private sectors of education. The role of the second of these needs some amplification. With the exception of that undertaken at maintained grammar schools, all the studies cited above included privately educated children as well as publicly educated ones. Private schools have been, and continue to be, a middle-class preserve; 'About 90 per cent of those at the private schools came from the service and intermediate classes' (Halsey *et al.*, 1980, p. 203). Moreover, it is a commonplace that they have on average greater resources per pupil than state schools. Hence the inequality in examination results between middle- and working-class children may in part reflect the differences in their relative consumption of private as well as public education.

But the apparently common sense proposition that inequality in the consumption of education leads to inequality in educational outcomes has recently been challenged. American sociologist Christopher Jencks and his associates at Harvard analysed a variety of statistical evidence concerning the relationship between educational consumption, usually measured by expenditure per pupil, and outcomes, measured by standard tests of cognitive skills. Their conclusions were that 'equalising the amount of schooling people get might reduce cognitive inequality among adults by 5 to 15 per cent'. However, far more important than education according to Jencks were genetic factors − 'if we could equalise everyone's genes, inequality in test scores would probably fall by 33 to 50 per cent' – and environmental ones – 'if we could equalise everyone's total environment, test score inequality would fall by 25 to 40 per cent' (Jencks, 1972, p. 109).

These results have been heavily criticised. In particular, they have been attacked on the grounds that the measures used, of both outcomes and consumption, were unsatisfactory. For instance, Michael Rutter *et al.* (1979), in their recent study *Fifteen Thousand Hours*, have concluded that, if more sophisticated measures are used, differences in consumption can be shown to make a difference to examination results. Even the critics, however, acknowledge that inequality in education is never likely to be more than a minor determinant of inequality in outcomes. Rutter *et al.* emphasise that they do not claim 'that schools are the *most* important influence on children's progress' (p. 182). Most researchers would argue that it is ultimately the socio-economic background of a child that will determine the bundle of educational skills he or she will acquire, partly because that background will affect the amount of education received in the manner discussed in the previous section, and partly because it will influence it directly through the effect on motivation and opportunities for study out of school.

Occupational mobility

With occupational mobility as with educational qualifications, it is a study from the Oxford Social Mobility Project which has provided the most recent comprehensive data (although again only for men). John Goldthorpe and his associates have used the Oxford sample to estimate the chances of an individual being found in a different occupational class from that of his father. A selection of their results is shown in Table 4.3. The second, third and fourth columns show, for men in three different age cohorts, the chances of their being found in the service class, relative to the chances of the sons of working-class fathers. It can be seen that in each cohort the relative chances of the son of a service-class father being himself in the service class was nearly four times that of the son of a working-class father. Thus, not only are the chances of 'getting to the top' much greater for those with fathers already at the top, but they have not altered significantly over time. The fifth, sixth and seventh columns show for men in each cohort the chances in 1972 of their being found in the working class relative to those of the sons of service-class fathers. In this case, the dis-

Table 4.3 *Relative Mobility by Occupational Class*

Men					England and Wales	
Occupational class of father	Relative chances of being found in 1972 in service class[a]			Relative chances of being found in 1972 in working class[b]		
	1908–17 cohort	1918–27 cohort	1928–37 cohort	1908–17 cohort	1918–27 cohort	1928–37 cohort
Service class	3.90	3.73	3.89	1.00	1.00	1.00
Intermediate class	1.75	1.89	1.98	2.18	2.19	2.50
Working class	1.00	1.00	1.00	3.29	3.71	4.47

[a] Relative to the chances of the sons of working-class fathers.
[b] Relative to the chances of the sons of service-class fathers.
Source: Goldthorpe (1980, p. 75, Table 3.2).

parity has actually increased over time, with the sons of working-class fathers in the first cohort being three times as likely to be in the working class themselves as the sons of service-class fathers, compared with over four-and-a-half times for the third cohort.

The researchers conclude that 'the pattern of relative mobility chances ... that has been associated with the British class structure over recent decades embodies inequalities that are of a quite striking kind. In particular, an enormous discrepancy emerges if one compares the chances of men whose fathers held higher-level service class positions being themselves found in such positions rather than working-class ones with the same relative chances of men who are of working-class origins.' Further, despite the fact that over the period to which the data relate there was large-scale educational reform and expansion, 'no significant reduction in class inequalities has in fact been achieved ... Relative mobility rates have remained generally unaltered; and the only trends that may arguably be discerned ... are indeed ones that would point to a widening of differences in class chances' (Goldthorpe, 1980, p. 252).

Goldthorpe's data are taken from a period when selective schools predominated; and it is possible that the spread of comprehensivisation since then has made some difference. But evidence from the United States (which has already had a form of comprehensive system) suggests that any such hope may be too optimistic. De Lone, reviewing the available evidence, argued that the US 'social structure appears no more fluid than that of other industrialized nations. The historian Stephan Thernstrom, reviewing evidence on occupational mobility from one generation to the next ... over the past century and a half, has concluded that the inequalities in life chances associated with social class have altered scarcely at all ... (a conclusion) entirely consistent with findings of the great bulk of studies that have looked at intergenerational mobility in the United States in the twentieth century' (de Lone, 1979, pp. 14–15). Jencks, in his most recent work on the subject, concluded that 'background exerts a larger influence on economic outcomes than past research has suggested, accounting for something like 48 per cent of the variance in occupational status ... If our aim is to reduce the impact of being born to one set of parents rather than another, we still have a long way to go' (1979, pp. 229–30).

Earnings

There are two kinds of educational outcome with respect to earnings that could be investigated. One, in line with the discussions of educational qualifications and occupations, is to examine the proportion of people from different social and economic backgrounds in different earnings strata. Unfortunately, there seems to be little information on this, for Britain at least. The other is to examine inequality in the distribution of earnings itself (the parallel in the educational qualifications case would be to examine inequality in the overall distribution of qualifications; there is no parallel in the case of occupational mobility). Here there are more data.

The most comprehensive investigation of the distribution of earnings in the UK has been done by Guy Routh (1980).[12] He presents data on earnings in eight different occupational classifications, from 1913–14 up until 1978. A small selection of his results are shown in Table 4.4. From that table it can be seen that in 1978 men in those classes roughly corresponding to the top SEGs (higher professionals and managers) had on average earnings one-and-a-half times the mean and well over twice those of those corresponding to the bottom SEGs (semi- and unskilled). However, the dispersion appears to have reduced over time. For instance, in 1960 the top groups were earning nearly twice the mean and nearly four times as much as the bottom groups; and the differences were greater then than in 1922–4.

It is tempting to ascribe this apparent reduction in the dispersion of earnings over the past fifty years to the expansion of both

Table 4.4 *Average Pay by Occupational Class: Percentage of Mean*

Men			Great Britain
Occupational class	1922–4	1960	1978
Higher professionals	206	195	159
Lower professionals[a]	113	81	104
Managers	169	177	154
Clerks	64	65	71
Foremen	95	97	90
Skilled manual	64	76	83
Semi-skilled manual	44	56	73
Unskilled manual	45	51	65
Mean (£) = 100	283.2	1042.5	5216.0

[a] Teachers, nurses, etc.

Source: Routh (1980, p. 127, Table 2.30).

compulsory and non-compulsory education in that period. Raising the age after which people can leave school creates greater equality in amounts of overall education received by the children of different social groups, and hence may create greater equality in their earnings. That this effect may be significant is suggested in a study by Blaug, Dougherty and Psacharopoulos (1980) of the effects of raising the school leaving age in 1972; their results indicate that the dispersion of earnings may have been reduced by as much as 15 per cent. An expansion of further and higher education has the effect of increasing the supply of people with certain qualifications relative to those without, a factor which would be expected to bring down the earnings of the former relative to the latter, as indeed Routh's evidence suggests has actually occurred.

But there is an important caveat. Both those arguments require that the agent of causation of changes in the distribution of earnings be changes in the distribution of education. A necessary condition for this to be correct is that the amount of education an individual receives affects his or her level of earnings, either through raising productivity or, as it is now fashionable to argue, by simply acting as a signal to employers that the individual concerned has relatively high ability. This proposition has been challenged by, again, Christopher Jencks (1972) who argued on the basis of evidence from a wide variety of sources that differences in income were not systematically correlated with differences in education. This contradicts the evidence from a number of other studies (for instance, Psacharopoulos, 1977a); and in a more recent work using different evidence Jencks has retreated somewhat from this position, acknowledging that his conclusions in this respect were possibly 'premature' (1979, p. 311). None the less, the exact nature of the link between education and earnings is still something of an open question; and hence so is the link between inequalities in education and in earnings.

Equality and Policy

A concern for the promotion of equality in some form appears in nearly all the major government statements and official reports on educational policy since the Second World War.[13] It has permeated the writings of social reformers and commentators on the subject. But there have been curiously few attempts to see whether equality of any kind has actually been achieved. Has the vast expansion of education since the war achieved the hope of its egalitarian supporters? And, if not, what can be done about it?

Objectives

In order to compare an actual distribution with any egalitarian objective in a useful fashion, it is necessary to have some precise specification of the latter. But this is not easy to find. The kinds of equality advocated vary from report to report and reformer to reformer. Most, however, are variants on the themes of 'equality of educational opportunity' and 'equality of outcome'. What follows is an attempt to specify these particular terms more precisely.

There appear to be four principal interpretations of equality of educational opportunity. The first is in terms of equality of access (Halsey, 1972, p. 6), a conception implied in, for instance, the Robbins Report's 'axiom' that 'courses of higher education should be available for all who are qualified by ability and attainment to pursue them and who wish to do so' (*Higher Education*, p. 8). As was argued in Chapter 2, equality of access can in turn best be understood as implying *equality of cost*, an objective achieved if all individuals regardless of their social background face the same private cost for each 'unit' of education undertaken.[14]

The second interpretation requires that 'each individual should receive an equal share of educational resources' (Evetts, 1970, p. 427). This is a form of *equality of use*, that is, each individual should use educational resources to the same extent. A third interpretation is 'to treat all those children of the same measured ability the same way' (*ibid.*). This is again a form of equality of use, with the relevant individuals being defined this time not as all individuals in the population but as individuals of equal ability.

The fourth interpretation is best expressed by Halsey (1972, p. 8), viz.:

> A society affords equal educational opportunity if the proportion of people from different social, economic or ethnic categories at all levels and in all types of education are more or less the same as the proportion of those people in the population at large ... i.e. ... the *average* woman or negro or proletarian or rural dweller should have the same level of educational attainment as the average male, white, white-collar suburbanite.

This is also a form of equality of use, although, in this case, it is equality of use per head between social groups.[15] It should be noted that, if ability were distributed equally between the various social categories, then this interpretation would be consistent with equal use for equal ability, but not necessarily with equal use for all. For instance, suppose that (1) 10 per cent of both manual and non-manual families had the ability to go to university and (2) that they did in fact attend university, then equality of educational opportunity would have been achieved in the senses of equality of use between the 'average' members of the occupational classes and of equal use for equal ability; but there would not, of course, be equality of use across all individuals.

These interpretations could be confined to the public sector. That is, equality of educational opportunity could be taken to imply either equal use of the public sector by all individuals (or by those of equal ability), or equal use of the public sector per head for different groups. If use of the public sector is measured by public expenditure, then that would imply *equality of public expenditure* either between all individuals (or those of equal ability) or per head between groups. This last interpretation seems implicit in several recent court decisions in the United States requiring states to equalise their educational expenditures across ethnic groups, such as, for instance, *Serrano vs. Priest* in California (usefully discussed in Friedman and Wiseman, 1978).

As with equality of educational opportunity, there are competing interpretations of *equality of outcome*. Here the differences concern not only whether all individuals or just the 'average member' of a social group is considered, but also the indicator of outcome used, such as educational qualifications, occupations or earnings. One interpretation, paralleling the second definition of equality of educational opportunity, is in terms of equality of outcome between all individuals, an interpretation which, it may be noted, only makes sense in terms of educational qualifications and earnings. Horace Mann, quoted at the beginning of this chapter as describing education as 'the great equalizer of the conditions of man', was presumably using this interpretation (with particular respect to earnings) for he went on to argue that 'it does better to disarm the poor of their hostility towards the rich; it prevents being poor' (quoted in de Lone, 1979, p. 42).

Another interpretation, paralleling the fourth definition of equality of educational opportunity, is in terms of equality of outcome between the average members of different social groups. That is, equality of outcome is achieved if the proportions of people from different social backgrounds with a given outcome are the same. In this case, the indicator could be any of the three possibilities: educational qualifications, earnings or occupation.

The reader may by now be feeling slightly confused by this proliferation of different notions of educational equality. It may help to summarise briefly the conceptions discussed. There seem to be four basic interpretations of the objective of equality in the field of education: equality of use of the education system; equality of the private cost per unit of use; equality of public expenditure on education; and equality of the outcome of education, defined variously in terms of educational qualifications, occupation or earnings. Each of these may refer either to equality between all individuals, between all individuals of the same ability or between the average members of different social groups.

Reality

The next task is to compare the distributions implied by some of those interpretations with those that have actually been observed, as outlined earlier in the chapter. The interpretations investigated are equality of public expenditure, cost and use between social groups; equality of outcome (educational qualifications and occupation) between social groups; and equality of outcome (earnings) between individuals. It should be noted that if the existence of inequality is established between social groups then this of course implies that inequality also exists across individuals; hence most of the possible combinations are being examined.

To begin with equality of public expenditure. The richest fifth of the income distribution receives nearly three times as much expenditure per household than the poorest fifth. These figures are partly influenced by differences in household size and in the age structure of the income groups, but it is unlikely that adjusting for such differences would wholly or even largely eliminate the inequality. If the population is divided by occupation instead of by income, a similar picture emerges. The top socio-economic group (professionals, employers and managers) receives nearly 50 per cent more public expenditure on education per person in the relevant age range than the bottom group (semi- and unskilled manual workers). Within those totals, the top group receives slightly less expenditure on primary and secondary education for pupils under 16 than the bottom group; but it benefits from nearly twice as much for secondary pupils over 16, over three times as much for further education and over five times as much for university education. These figures also suggest that equality of use has not been achieved either. Because of the existence of private education, the distribution of the use of the education system (both public and private) will be more unequal than the distribution of public expenditure on education. Hence the fact of substantial inequality in public expenditure suggests that there is an even greater inequality in use. Moreover, there is evidence to suggest that these inequalities have remained largely constant over the last fifty years.

Inequalities of cost also persist. Despite the provision of free education and the expansion of the student awards system, the lower income groups face greater financial costs in keeping children at school past the school-leaving age than the higher groups. Although this is reversed for university education, the costs in terms of sacrifice may still be greater for low income than for high income households. Indeed, as Psacharopoulos (1977b) has pointed out, subsidising higher education may even have made things worse for working-class students. Lowering the price of education will, other things being equal, raise the number of aspirants relative to the number of places available. As a result, entrance to higher education becomes more competitive; better A-level results are required to enter university, for instance. This actually improves the chances of the candidate from a middle-class background relative to one from the working class, since the former are in a better position to prepare for, and hence do well in, the relevant exams. Hence the subsidy to higher education, although lowering the cost to working-class students in one sense (through reducing the cost once they are at college), simultaneously raises the costs elsewhere (through increasing the amount of preparation that has to be done). The net effect may be actually to increase costs, and hence discourage working-class participation.

Halsey *et al.* (1980, pp. 69–70) make a similar point in the context of subsidising secondary education.

> By increasing the subsidy ... the state may have tempted some parents of able children to forsake the private sector of education for the state one, and the extra competition from these children may thus have nullified any gains which the working class would otherwise have obtained from the reforms. The point is an important and paradoxical one for social policy. A service is made free in order to enable the poor to take advantage of it, but this also makes the service more attractive to the rich.

Nor has equality of outcome been achieved. There remain considerable inequalities in educational qualifications and occupational mobility between social groups. In 1972 12 per cent of sons with working-class fathers had O-levels, 7 per cent had A-levels and only 5 per cent a degree; the comparable figures for the middle class were 50, 25 and 20 per cent, respectively. As far as occupation is concerned, the chance of a son of the middle class finding an occupation in the middle class was four times the chance of working-class sons finding themselves in the middle class; the middle-class sons had also less than a quarter the chance of becoming working class relative to those from the working class. Moreover, there is little sign of any improvement over time. The gap between the proportion of the working and middle classes going to university has actually widened over the last fifty years. The relative chances of boys with middle- or working-class fathers of themselves getting into the middle class have remained virtually constant over the same period, while the gap between their chances of becoming working class has actually increased.

If inequality in outcome is measured in terms of dispersion in earnings across individuals, then inequality persists here as well. Higher professionals and managers earn nearly two-and-a-half times more than semi- and unskilled manual workers. There has been some improvement over time, with the dispersion falling somewhat over the past fifty years, but the extent to which this is attributable to the expansion of education is not settled.

Prospects for Policy

Overall it seems that public expenditure on education has failed as a means of achieving equality. In none of its interpretations has equality of educational opportunity been reached; nor has equality of outcome been attained (except perhaps in terms of slightly greater equality of earnings). But what are the implications of this for policy? Does it imply that public expenditure on education should be curtailed or even eliminated altogether, particularly in those areas where the greatest inequality exists, such as non-compulsory education? Or might there be changes in the system of publicly financed education which could promote greater equality while keeping the basic principles of the present system intact?

As in the case of the NHS, the effects on inequality of reducing, or eliminating, expenditure on education after the school-leaving age depend on how the tax revenues thus released were used. If they were used to increase the cash incomes of the poor, the result would be greater equality in final income, because (so long as other things remained equal) a pro-rich element of such income would be replaced by a pro-poor one. There might be greater equality of use, because, although costs of attending institutions of higher education would rise for both higher and lower social groups, the lower groups would now have (relatively) higher incomes to meet those costs. Indeed, if the point made by Psacharopoulos and Halsey *et al.* is correct concerning the effects of subsidisation on competition, the result might even be an overall reduction in working-class costs.

It might be noted that much of the above remains true even if the tax revenues released were used in less progressive ways. For instance, suppose the public subsidy to universities was eliminated, and the taxes of the rich as well as the poor were reduced. Then there would only be greater inequality in final income if the absolute value of reduction in tax payments by the top SEG was over *five times* that of the lowest SEG. For any ratio less than that, the lowest group would be better off as a result of the change and the highest group less well off.

Overall it seems that there is a strong case on egalitarian grounds for reducing the subsidies to education beyond the school-leaving age. Against this, however, it could be argued that these subsidies serve purposes other than equality. In particular, the nation needs well educated people in order to have good managers, engineers, civil servants and so on, and hence should be prepared to pay for their education. But even if it is accepted (and it is by no means uncontroversial) that higher education does create more productive individuals, this argument is dubious. For if society values good managers and engineers, then this should be reflected in the incomes that such people can command. If individuals have their productivity increased by their education, then, other things being equal, their employers will pay them higher wages. There is little element of what economists call 'external benefit' here: no provision of a service without compensation. Rather there is the normal process of market exchange with people receiving extra income in return for the extra service they provide.

Are there any arguments on egalitarian grounds for increasing, rather than reducing, public expenditure on education? One suggestion is the extension of the means-tested student grants system to cover those who stay on at school after 16. This would reduce the costs faced by prospective working-class students relative to middle-class students and might thereby decrease inequalities in use. But, given the magnitude of all the factors discouraging working-class use, it is difficult to imagine such grants being introduced on a large enough scale to have a very significant impact.

Increasing public expenditure on the compulsory sector has more in its favour. Raising the school-leaving age, for example, would increase the ratio of compulsory (broadly equally distributed) education to non-compulsory (highly unequally distributed) education and hence distribute public expenditure and use more equally (see Psacharopoulos, 1981). It might also have an effect on other aspects of inequality; for instance, the research by Blaug *et al.* (1980) mentioned earlier suggests that it might reduce the dispersion of earnings.

On balance, however, it is difficult to resist the impression that by and large public expenditure on education is not really an effective tool for promoting equality. Other observers have come to similar conclusions. French sociologist Raymond Boudon in a comprehensive review of the evidence across many countries, both West and East, argues that 'society rather than school is responsible for IEO [inequality of education opportunity]', (1974, p. 114), drawing the conclusion that changing the system of schooling will have little effect on either educational opportunity or on wider social and economic inequality. Jencks agrees, claiming that 'there is no evidence that school reform can substantially reduce the extent of cognitive inequality' (1972, p. 8), and hence that 'school reform will not achieve a reduction in wider social and economic inequalities either' (1979, p. 311).[16] De Lone uses a comprehensive discussion of the American evidence to argue similarly (1979, p. 112).

The ability of public expenditure on education to achieve equality appears to be limited, however the latter is defined. The provision of free education has created neither equality of use, cost, public expenditure nor outcome. Indeed, it is possible that in some cases it may actually have promoted greater inequality. The reason for this appears to be the pervasive influence of the structure of broader social and economic inequality, a structure that itself seems largely impervious to educational reform.

Notes to Chapter 4

1   Appendix B, Table B.1.
2   *The Government's Expenditure Plans*, which form the basis of Figure 4.1, do not give a breakdown of capital expenditure between primary, secondary and other schools. The statements in the text concerning capital expenditure on these items are based on 1977/8 estimates published in Department of Education and Science (1979, Table 2, pp. 4–6).
3   Rogers also includes a number of other items as part of the public subsidy to independent schools, including the payment of school fees for the children of those in the armed forces and the diplomatic staff, local

authority payments of independent school fees for certain children and the state training of teachers subsequently employed in those schools. Of these, the first is more correctly regarded as a supplement to the wages of the personnel involved (and hence part of public expenditure in that area); the second, as part of the expenditure on 'other schools'; and the third, as part of the expenditure on further education.

4   The Family Expenditure Survey is carried out annually by the Department of Employment. It was originally designed to obtain data for constructing the weights in the Retail Price Index, but it is now used for a wide variety of other purposes. It samples about 7,000 households (20,000 people) and provides data on their income and private expenditure (business expenditure is not included).

5   These are published annually. See, for instance, Department of Education and Science (1979, p. 25, Table 12).

6   According to the 1978 FES, the average number of persons per household in the lowest fifth of the income distribution in 1978 was 1.46, compared with 2.85 for the middle three-fifths and 3.57 for the highest fifth (Department of Employment, 1979, p. 15, Table E). Income here is gross income (see Appendix C) rather than original income.

7   Pechman went on to compare the benefits received by each group with the taxes they paid, and concluded that the *net* effect was actually pro-poor. Judy (1970) has claimed a similar result for Canada. But this does not seem a legitimate procedure. Since some of the tax revenues in each case are spent on services other than higher education, the benefits from those services should also be included in any calculation of the net effects. See Peacock (1974) for a similar point in the context of the CSO studies.

Hansen and Weisbrod's original study has also been criticised by McGuire (1976) for omitting student financial aid. He goes on to produce estimates to show that if such aid is included the effect of the system is pro-poor. Unfortunately, as with Hansen and Weisbrod's original results, these are not presented in a manner compatible with the other material in this chapter; hence they cannot be directly evaluated. See also Hansen and Weisbrod (1978) and McGuire (1978).

8   Estimates of the distribution of public expenditure on education are included in the aggregate studies of the distribution of taxes and public expenditure in the 1930s, 1940s and 1950s listed in Appendix A (p. 155). But these are generally not based on actual data concerning use, but on simple *a priori* assumptions (e.g. that each child in each income group received the same educational expenditure).

9   For an analysis similar to that which follows, see Gary Becker's Woytinski lecture (1975, pp. 94–144).

10 This may be so even if, as has been argued by Papanicolaou and Psacharopoulos (1979), the *actual* benefits, as measured by the rate of return to education, are larger for the lower groups than the higher ones.

11 Among the proponents of this view are Schneider and Lysgaard (1953) and Sugarman (1970). Inability to defer gratification is also included as one of the characteristics of Lewis' Culture of Poverty (see, e.g., Lewis, 1966, p. xlvii). For more sceptical sociological views, see Miller, Riessman and Seagull (1965) and Allen (1970).

12 A useful discussion of the principal sources of data and of the patterns they reveal can be found in the Royal Commission on the Distribution of Income and Wealth's eighth report (1979).

13 See, for example, the White Paper that preceded the 1944 Education Act (*Educational Reconstruction*, 1943, p. 3); the Robbins Report (*Higher Education*, 1963, p. 8); Edward Boyle's preface to the Newsom Report on secondary education (Ministry of Education, 1963, p. iv); the Plowden Report on nursery education (Department of Education and Science, 1967, p. 1).

14 This is also how Becker (1975, p. 123) interprets equality of opportunity.

15 The term 'attainment' in Halsey's quote is slightly ambiguous; it could refer to educational skills or qualifications (outcomes, in my terminology) rather than use. But it seems clear from the preceding sentence that use is implied.

16 In the earlier work (1972) he came to the same conclusion. But in that case it was based not just on the proposition that school reform cannot equalise cognitive inequality but also that, even if it could, such equalisation would have little effect on the occupational and income distributions. As noted above, he is now less certain of the second proposition; hence in the later study (1979) he rests his case largely on the first.

CHAPTER 5

Housing

The Government's housing objectives are:

(i) a decent home for every family at a price within their means;

(ii) a fairer choice between owning a home and renting one;

(iii) fairness between one citizen and another in giving and receiving help towards housing costs. *Fair Deal for Housing*, Cmnd 4728

State involvement in housing has grown steadily since the passing of the Public Health Acts in the nineteenth century. Currently there are a wide variety of programmes requiring direct public expenditure, including the provision of council housing at subsidised rents, rent allowances to private tenants, option mortgages, payments to housing associations and improvement grants for house owners. In 1978–9 these cost the public budget over £5,000 million – 8 per cent of total public expenditure and the fifth largest item.[1] There are also sizeable tax expenditures associated with housing, that is, tax reliefs, primarily for owner-occupiers, which reduce the government's tax revenue below the level that would obtain in their absence, and hence have an impact on the overall government budget equivalent to the more conventional direct expenditures. Calculation of the sums involved depends on how the relevant tax expenditures are defined, but one estimate puts the 1978–9 figure at nearly £3,000 million.[2]

Public subsidisation of housing has been justified on a number of grounds, including the promotion of social efficiency and the attainment of minimum standards. But there has also been concern that such subsidisation is 'fair', that different groups in the population are treated equitably by the public expenditure system. Accordingly, it is important to establish the distributional impact of the system, and such is the task of this chapter.[3] Its structure differs slightly from those on health care and education in that the discussion of the distribution of public expenditure is divided into three separate sections (reflecting the emphasis in the literature): the distribution of direct expenditures, the distribution of tax expenditures and the impact of the whole system on housing costs. The remaining sections follow the pattern of the other chapters, being first concerned with the distribution of housing 'outcomes' and then with the relationship between the consequences of housing policies and the promotion of equality, and the prospects for reform.

A few points need to be made by way of preliminary. People live in all kinds of housing: detached, semi-detached and terraced houses, flats, caravans and so on. To avoid tedious repetition, where necessary these will be collectively referred to as houses. There are a variety of different kinds of public authority associated with the provision of public housing in the UK. Of these, by far the most important is the local authority or council which will be taken to refer to them all. Similarly, all public housing will be described as 'council' housing and its occupants as council tenants. The term 'tenure' may not be immediately familiar to those new to the housing field; it refers to the various forms of legal and financial arrangements under which the inhabitants of a house have the right to live in it, such as owner-occupation, renting from a private landlord or renting from a local authority. Finally, as mentioned in Chapter 2, it is difficult to distinguish between the 'use' and 'outcome' of the service in the case of housing; hence only outcomes are considered.

The Distribution of Direct Public Expenditure

There are many forms of direct public expenditure on housing, and, in order to make the subsequent discussion more comprehensible, it is necessary to provide some detail of the different types involved. Current expenditure on housing may be grouped into four basic categories: general subsidies, rent rebates and allowances, the option mortgage scheme and administration. *General subsidies* are funds which make up the difference between local authorities' current expenditures on council housing (supervision, maintenance and the servicing of housing related debt) and the nominal income they receive from rents (rent income before any rebates are taken into account). *Rent rebates and allowances* are refunds of rent to local authority tenants (rebates) and to private tenants (allowances). Both are means-tested, paying a proportion of the rent (as registered with the local rent office) for households with incomes below certain prescribed levels, the proportion of rent paid increasing with household size and decreasing with household income. In addition, all those receiving supplementary benefit are entitled to have their rent paid; a sum equal to 60 per cent of the rents for those households is usually included as part of the total costs of the rent rebate scheme. The *option mortgage scheme* is designed to reduce mortgage interest payments for low income buyers who do not pay enough tax to qualify for the mortgage interest tax allowances; the *administration* category is self-explanatory.

Capital expenditure on housing is of three kinds: the building of council housing, improvement grants, and other grants and loans. The first is the total expenditure on the purchase of land and the construction of new dwellings, net of any income from sales. *Improvement grants* are grants made to private individuals for the purpose of improving their property. They include grants for the provision of standard amenities, for improving insulation and for certain other improvements at the local authority's discretion. *Other grants and loans* include net lending to private persons for house purchase and improvements, and various payments to housing associations.

The relative importance of the various categories in 1978–9 is illustrated in Figure 5.1. It is apparent that general expenditures on council housing took up by far the largest slice, both of current and capital expenditure: about 70 per cent of each. Most of the remainder of current expenditure was on rent rebates and allowances (over 20 per cent), while the rest of capital expenditure consisted of grants and loans to private persons (including improvement grants) or housing associations.

Estimates of the distribution of these expenditures have generally been confined to calculating the subsidy received by current council tenants. These are of two kinds: those using 'accounting-cost' estimates of the subsidy and those using 'opportunity-cost' estimates.[4] The meaning of these terms, and the

CURRENT   CAPITAL

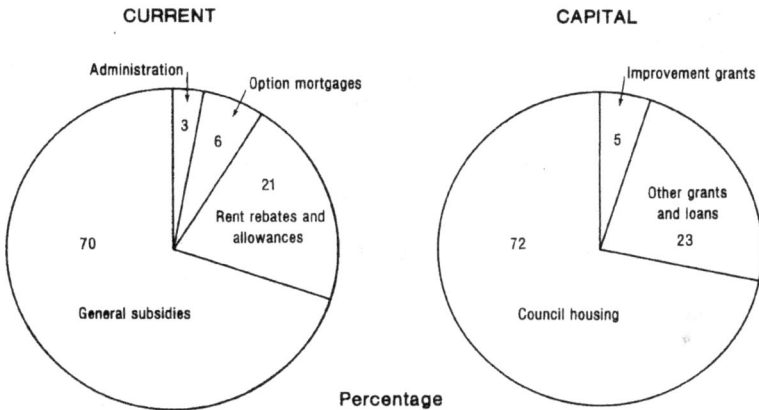

Percentage

Figure 5.1   Direct public expenditure on housing by category, Great
Britain 1978–9.
Source: Appendix B, Table B.2.

distinction between the studies, will become apparent shortly.
Both types of study present their results by households grouped
according to annual income; there are no estimates by income
group per person, or of occupational group per person or per
household. All assume that public expenditure on housing is
incident upon its nominal beneficiaries.[5]

Accounting-cost estimates are available in one of the Technical
Volumes that accompanied the 1977 Green Paper on Housing
Policy inspired by Crosland (Department of the Environment,
1977) and in the annual studies of the incidence of taxes and
benefits produced by the Central Statistical Office (CSO).[6] In both
cases, the methodology is similar and the CSO studies can
therefore be taken as representative. There the subsidy to each
local authority tenant is calculated as the difference between the
rent actually paid and a rent based on the cost of that house to the
local authority as reflected in its accounts (hence the name for the
procedure). The subsidy is thus the sum of the *general subsidy*
received by the household (the difference between the accounting
cost of the house and the nominal rent it is charged by the local
authority) and any *rent rebate* it receives (the difference, if any,
between the nominal rent and the actual rent paid). The rent paid
is taken from the Family Expenditure Survey. The accounting
cost is calculated as a proportion of the total current housing

expenditure by the local authority, the proportion being that of the rateable value of the house to that of the total rateable value of all dwellings owned by the authority.

Some recent estimates are summarised in Figure 5.2. It can be seen that in 1978 households in the bottom 20 per cent of the income distribution received on average nearly four times as much per household as those in the top 17 per cent. Interestingly, this is not because poor council tenants receive a better deal than wealthier ones; the Green Paper's Technical Volume estimates show that on average all council tenants receive roughly the same subsidy, with a slightly pro-rich general subsidy being offset by pro-poor rent rebates (Department of the Environment, 1977, p. 213, Table IV. 35). Rather, it arises because, contrary to popular myth, low income groups have a far higher proportion of council tenants than those with high incomes. For instance, in 1978 they comprised over half of the bottom fifth of the income distribution, compared with less than 20 per cent of the top fifth.[7]

Critics of these estimates have concentrated upon the use of accounting costs as the basis for estimating the relevant subsidy. Rather, they argue, the true cost of a local authority house is not the accounting cost, but the income the authority could have earned if it had invested its 'equity' – the capital locked up in the

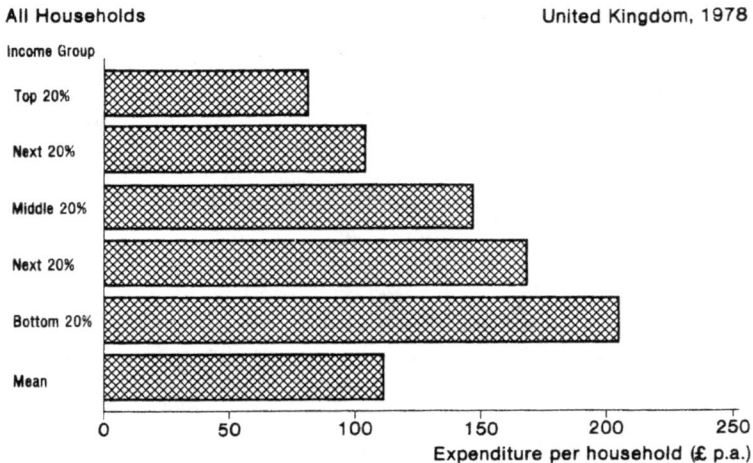

Figure 5.2   Direct public expenditure on council tenants by income group: Accounting-cost estimates.
Source: Appendix B, Table B.3.

house – in some other way. For instance, consider a council house costing, say, £100 in maintenance a year and £500 in interest paid on the bonds issued to finance it. If the authority rents it out for £200 a year, then, since the accounting cost is £600, the subsidy on an accounting cost basis is £400. But now suppose the market value of the house to be £10,000. The local authority could sell the house, invest the cash at, say, an after-tax rate of return of 10 per cent, and thereby increase its income by £1,000 a year. Thus the real cost to the council (and so to its ratepayers) of keeping the house and renting it out to the existing tenants is this 'opportunity cost' of £1,000 per year, plus the maintenance costs of £100 (but not the interest payments on the bonds, which would have to be paid anyway). Hence the true subsidy to the tenants is £900: the difference between the total cost of £1,100 and their rent (£200).

Estimates calculated on this basis have been produced by various economists, including L. Rosenthal of Keele (1977), Gordon Hughes of Cambridge (1979) and Ray Robinson of the University of Sussex (1980). The methodology of all three studies is similar; Robinson's may be taken as representative. His estimates are for 1977. He took the real cost of a dwelling to a local authority in that year to be the maintenance costs, plus the income that would have been earned if the equity locked up in the dwelling had been invested at a rate of return obtainable from substitute investment opportunities, such as government securities. Using data from the Family Expenditure Survey he calculated the difference between this cost and the rent actually paid by council tenants in different income groups. A selection of his results (adjusted to make them comparable with other material in this book) is shown in Table 5.1. The third column of that table gives the average subsidy received by council tenants in each group, expressed as a percentage of the mean. It can be seen that it is the poorer tenants who receive the larger subsidy, with those in the lowest income group receiving about 60 per cent more per household than those in the highest. The fourth column shows the distribution of the subsidy between households (tenant and non-tenant), giving the average subsidy per household as a percentage of the mean. As with the accounting-cost estimates, the distribution is markedly pro-poor, with households in the lowest group (about one fifth of the population) receiving over three times as much on average as those in the highest group

Table 5.1 Public Expenditure on Housing by Income Group

Great Britain, 1977

All households		Expenditure: percentage of mean					
		Council tenant subsidy		Owner-occupier subsidy		Total	
Income group[a] (p.a.)	Percentage of all households	Per tenant household	Per household	Per owner-occupier household[b]	Per household	per household	
£6,240 or more	26.5	78	54	147	191	156	
£4,160–£6,239	27.2	82	74	94	100	90	
£2,080–£4,159	25.0	96	116	86	66	86	
Less than £2,080	21.3	115	170	53	28	83	
Mean (£)	—	353	116	338	184	300	

[a] Gross income.

[b] Robinson's minimum estimate.

Source: Calculated from Robinson (1980, Tables 2–4; Department of Employment (1978, Table 1, pp. 18–21, Table 35, p. 94).

(about a quarter of the population). This is due partly to the fact that the poorer tenants get larger subsidies as we have seen, and partly to the higher proportion of council tenants in the lower income groups.

Although no estimates have been made of the distribution of subsidy by occupational group, it is likely that this too would favour the lowest groups. Table 5.2 shows the distribution of household tenure by socio-economic group. Over half of those in the lowest group are council tenants, compared with just 8 per cent in the highest group. Since each group contains approximately the same number of households, the average subsidy per household must also be greater for the lower groups. All in all, therefore, it seems as though council housing is one area of public expenditure that benefits primarily the lower social groups.

There is little evidence concerning the distribution of the other direct expenditures. Townsend found that the applicants for option mortgages were generally in the 'lowish though not lowest income groups' (1979, p. 879). Rent allowances, being means-tested, almost certainly favour the poor, but since only just over half of the eligible households take them up, they do not assist as much as they might.[8]

Improvement grants, on the other hand, almost certainly favour the better off. Christine Whitehead, housing economist at

Table 5.2   *Household Tenure by Socio-Economic Group*

All households					*Great Britain, 1978*
Socio-economic group		*Tenure*			
	Owner-occupied	*Rented from local authority*	*Rented privately*	*Other[a]*	*Base = 100 %*
	(%)	(%)	(%)	(%)	
Professionals, employers and managers	82	8	6	5	2194
Intermediate and junior non-manual	59	25	12	5	2444
Skilled manual	49	40	9	3	3682
Semi- and unskilled manual	29	56	11	3	2832

Note: Percentages may not add up because of rounding off.
[a] Rental with job or business, or from housing association or co-operative.
Source: Calculated from OPCS (1980, p. 34, Table 3.10(b)).

the London School of Economics, has argued that 'since there is almost no economic reason for private landlords to take up grants it is reasonable to assume that most grants went to existing owner-occupiers, and among them probably mainly to younger and better off households' (Whitehead, 1977, p. 46). This view is supported by the English House Conditions Survey which found 'some indication' that the principal beneficiaries of improvement grants were owner-occupiers on above average incomes (Department of the Environment, 1979, p. 21). It is possible that the existence of improvement grants may have been 'capitalised' in the prices of unimproved property. For instance, a poor old age pensioner may be able to sell his house to a young professional planning to improve it for a higher price than would have been possible if there had been no grants. None the less it seems reasonable to conclude that on balance the principal beneficiaries of improvement grants are in the higher social groups.

Finally, a brief word concerning the distribution of direct public expenditures on housing in other countries. The only evidence of which I am aware comes from a Brookings Institution study by Henry Aaron, who investigated the distribution of public housing subsidies in the United States by income group. He found that the subsidy accrued very largely to low income groups, but the subsidy per public tenant showed relatively little variation (1972, p. 122, Table 7-5), presumably because there was no rent rebate scheme comparable to the British one.

The Distribution of Tax Expenditures

Although less conspicuous than direct expenditures, the housing subsidies created by the tax system are no less important. These are housing-associated tax reliefs (particularly for owner-occupiers) whose impact on the public budget is exactly the same as if the household concerned had received cash grants instead. As such there is a general consensus that they should be viewed as part of the overall pattern of public expenditure on housing. In the British tax system, there are three main kinds of tax expenditures: owner-occupiers' exemption from capital gains tax when they sell their houses, mortgage interest tax relief and the absence of taxation of 'imputed income'. The first of these is self-explanatory; the second and third, which have to be viewed in conjunction with one another, need more explanation.

Under the tax system, the interest paid on a mortgage of £25,000 or less can be deducted from income before that income is assessed for tax. The original justification for this was that it was a part of a system for taxing 'imputed income'. This, and the rationale for taxing it, can be explained as follows. A house provides a flow of services: shelter, warmth, security, etc. It also has a flow of costs: rent, if the occupier is a tenant, or interest payments, among other things, if the occupier is buying it on a mortgage. The difference between the value of the services and costs can be viewed as income, though income in kind rather than in cash. That it is equivalent to money income can be inferred from the fact that in most cases one can be translated into the other quite easily. For instance, if the owner of a house decides to rent it out rather than live in it he will derive a cash income from the house equal to the difference between the rent he receives and the costs he pays on the house.

The fair way to treat this housing income for tax purposes would therefore be to tax it in a manner similar to other income. Anyone paying costs less than the value of the flow of housing services received is receiving 'income' and should pay tax on it in the normal way. And, until twenty years ago, this was the case in Britain. The Inland Revenue assessed a value of housing income for each owner-occupier, allowed him to deduct costs, including mortgage interest payments, and taxed the remainder. In 1963, largely for political reasons, the taxation of imputed income was stopped. However, the deduction of mortgage interest payments was permitted to continue – although its rationale had disappeared.

Those estimating the distribution of tax expenditures are thus left with two choices: either to treat the non-taxation of imputed income as a tax expenditure (but not the deduction of mortgage interest payments), or to ignore imputed income and simply consider the mortgage interest deduction as the tax expenditure.[9] Either way, the sums involved are considerable. The revenue lost through the mortgage interest deduction has been estimated for 1978–9 as £1,110 million (Board of Inland Revenue, 1979, Table 1.10, p. 15). Willis and Hardwick (1978, p. 93) estimated the revenue loss through the non-taxation of imputed income as £931 million in 1974–5, and the Meade Report estimated it as £1,500 million in 1976 (Meade, 1978, p. 519). To put these figures into perspective it should be noted that they are broadly comparable with the £1,872 million in 1978–9 for direct public expenditure on general subsidies (Appendix B, Table B.2).

Using data on income and mortgage payments from the Family Expenditure Survey, the authors of a paper in one of the Technical Volumes accompanying the Housing Policy Green Paper estimated the distribution of the combined effects of the mortgage interest deduction and the option mortgage subsidy between owner-occupiers. These showed a distribution that favoured the wealthier owner-occupier, with those households with heads earning £6,000 or more in 1974–5 receiving over six times as much on average per household as those earning £1,000 or less (Department of the Environment, 1977, p. 214, Table IV. 37). Willis and Hardwick have produced more aggregated estimates (1978, Table 8.6, pp. 99–100), showing a similar distributional pattern.

Such a distribution is hardly surprising. Tax rates rise with income and the value of a tax relief increases with the tax rate applied to income. For instance, consider two households with identical mortgage interest payments of £1,000 p.a. but one facing a marginal tax rate (the tax rate applied to any extra income received) of 30 per cent, and the other, by virtue of having a higher income, facing a marginal tax rate of 40 per cent. Both would be able to reduce their taxable income by £1,000, but the poorer household would thereby only reduce its tax bill by £300, whereas the other would reduce its taxes by £400. Hence the value of the tax deduction to the richer household is greater than that to the poorer one. When to this is added the fact that, in practice, wealthy households are likely to have larger mortgages than poor households, the explanation for the pro-rich distribution of this tax expenditure can be readily perceived.

Estimates of the distribution of the tax expenditures due to the non-taxation of imputed incomes and capital gains have been made by Hughes (1979) and Robinson (1980). Again we take Robinson's work as representative.[10] He calculated the distribution of the tax expenditures arising from the non-taxation of imputed income and capital gains for owner-occupiers in 1977. Imputed income was set equal to the return owner-occupiers would have received if their equity in the house had been invested elsewhere at a rate on a par with that for government securities;

liability for capital gains taxation was calculated by assuming that house prices rose at a given annual rate, and that owner-occupiers were taxed either on all of this gain (maximum estimate) or on half of it (minimum estimate).

Some of the results incorporating the minimum estimate are shown in Table 5.1. The fifth column of that table shows the subsidy per owner-occupier household and the sixth the subsidy per household (owner-occupiers and non-owner-occupiers). As with the mortgage interest estimates both of these are pro-rich, with owner-occupiers in the highest income group receiving nearly three times as much as those in the lowest group, and all households in the highest group receiving an average subsidy over six times as much as those in the lowest. Nor is this surprising. Wealthier owner-occupiers will tend to have larger houses, with therefore a greater flow of imputed income; they also generally face higher tax rates. Both of those factors imply that wealthier owner-occupiers will benefit from a larger subsidy due to the non-taxation of imputed income than poorer ones. In turn, this fact, coupled with the higher proportion of owner-occupiers in the higher income groups, explains why the higher income groups have a higher average subsidy per household.

Now it could be argued that results such as these are misleading (see Kay and King, 1978, pp. 61–2). It is possible that some owner-occupiers are not the chief beneficiaries of these tax expenditures, for the very existence of the tax expenditures may have raised the prices they had to pay for their homes. Indeed, if the supply of housing is totally unresponsive to price (if the supply of housing is totally inelastic, in technical language), then the effect of introducing a tax expenditure is simply to raise the price of houses *pari passu*, a once-and-for-all gain to those lucky enough to own houses at that time (and their descendants) but with no subsequent gains to anyone else.

Three points may be made in this connection. First, the supply of housing is not totally inelastic (see Robinson, 1980, pp. 8–9). Hence there will be some benefit accruing to existing owner-occupiers. Second, the argument depends on the reference point chosen. For it might be as plausible to argue that existing owner-occupiers are the principal beneficiaries of the tax expenditures since, if the expenditures were eliminated tomorrow and if supply were totally unresponsive to price, then they would be the principal losers. Third, it is unlikely that considerations of this sort alter the distributional pattern. Even if the absolute amount of benefit to existing owner-occupiers is actually less than the estimates indicate, their distribution is still likely to be pro-rich.

There are no studies of the distribution of tax expenditures by occupational group. But again the likely pattern can be inferred from the distribution of tenure by socio-economic group shown in Table 5.2. The proportion of owner-occupiers in the highest socio-economic group is far larger than in the lowest: over 80 per cent for the top group, compared with less than 30 per cent for the bottom group. Moreover, the owner-occupiers in the top group are likely to have a higher income on average than those in the bottom one, and therefore to have a higher average subsidy. Hence we could expect a distributional pattern of tax expenditures that favours — probably to a very considerable extent — the higher socio-economic groups.

Owner-occupiers are not the only beneficiaries of tax expenditures. Hughes (1979) points out that both public and private tenants may also benefit from the non-taxation of housing income if, as is often the case, they pay rent at less than the value of the housing services they receive. He has calculated the distribution of this benefit by income group. It is broadly neutral, with the exception of the very highest and lowest income groups (who both receive less than the remainder).

Evidence from abroad supports the conclusion that tax expenditures generally favour the better off. Aaron (1972), in the Brookings study already mentioned, estimated the distribution of tax expenditures in the United States. His calculations differed in a number of ways from the British work. In particular, he included deduction for property taxes (permitted under the US income tax, though not under the British), and also added together the tax expenditures due to the mortgage interest deduction and the non-taxation of imputed income. This last seems incorrect because, as argued earlier, if imputed income is to be taxed, then mortgage interest payments are a legitimate tax deduction. Not surprisingly, his results showed a similar pattern to that for Britain, with a distribution that is strongly pro-rich. Judith Yates (1979) of the University of Sydney calculated the distributional impact of subsidies arising from the non-taxation of imputed income in Australia for 1966 to 1968. Again the results showed a subsidy whose absolute value increases with income.

Finally, what is the overall distribution of public housing expenditure (both direct and through the tax system) in Britain? With the gaps in the data and with the variety of different estimates, it is difficult to give precise figures. But it is possible to combine Robinson's estimates for the two biggest subsidies – those to tenants and to owner-occupiers. This is done in the last column of Table 5.1. The result is an overall subsidy increasing gently with income until the highest income group is reached, when it jumps sharply.[11] These estimates omit rent allowances, tax subsidies to private tenants and improvement grants. While rent allowances benefit the less well off, tax subsidies to private tenants are neutral and improvement grants favour the better off. On balance, it seems unlikely that their inclusion would alter the overall pattern of distribution, one that favours better-off owner occupiers and hence again the higher income and socio-economic groups.

The Distribution of Costs

Not surprisingly, the difference in public subsidy detailed in the previous sections creates differences in the private cost per 'unit' of housing that each household faces. Professors Atkinson and King of the CLARE group of economists have recently produced an important analysis of the way in which money housing costs vary between different groups in the population (King and Atkinson, 1980); much of the following is based on their analysis.[12]

The cost of housing services to a tenant is simple to specify: his rent plus any maintenance expenses he had to bear. The cost of a house to an owner-occupier is more complex to assess. It has several components. First, there is the opportunity cost of his 'equity', that is, the income (after tax) he could receive if he took the capital he has invested in the house and invested it in some other form, such as government securities. Then the cost of any mortgage he has must be taken into account, that is, the interest payments on the mortgage, less any tax relief he received on those payments, plus the costs of maintenance. But this is not the complete picture. All of these increase his costs, but there is another factor which decreases it. House owners have an asset whose value increases over time. Hence they make capital gains,

which offset in whole or in part the other items of cost.
To summarise, the cost of housing services to an owner-occupier consists of the after-tax return on alternative investment of his equity, *plus* the after-tax interest payments on any mortgage, *plus* maintenance costs *minus* any capital gain. An algebraic formulation is given in a note.[13]

Now these costs will vary according to the owner-occupier's marginal tax rate (the rate of tax he pays on any extra income he receives) and the size of his mortgage. King and Atkinson have calculated these costs for a variety of different cases. Some of their estimates, adjusted to include average maintenance costs for owner occupiers, are shown in Table 5.3.

Table 5.3   *Annual Housing Costs to Owner-Occupier of £10,000 House*

Annual Housing Costs (£'s)				United Kingdom, 1977
Percentage of value of house mortgaged	Marginal tax rate of owner-occupiers (%)			
	30	40	50	60
80%	202	76	− 50	− 176
20%	328	184	40	− 104

Note: Mortage interest rates assumed to be 12 per cent; rate of increase of house prices, 8 per cent; opportunity cost of owner's equity, 15 per cent; average annual maintenance costs for owner-occupiers, £120 (Department of Employment, 1978, Table 1, p. 21); mortgages below £25,000 ceiling.
Source: Calculated from King and Atkinson (1980, p. 10, Table 3).

From this table it is immediately apparent that costs are less, the larger the mortgage and the tax rate. Indeed, some of the cases illustrated (such as those with an 80 per cent mortgage facing 50 or 60 per cent marginal tax rates) actually have *negative* costs; in other words, they are being paid to live in their accommodation.

Moreover, these costs are almost certainly less than the costs of living as a tenant, either of a local authority or a private landlord. Robinson (1980) estimated the average value of a council house in England and Wales in 1977 to be approximately £10,000, and its average rent as about £400. The Family Expenditure Survey for that year estimates the average annual expenditure on repairs and maintenance for local authority tenants to be £27 (Department of Employment, 1978, Table 1, p. 21). Hence the total cost to the average local tenant of a house worth £10,000 was £427, a figure likely to be greater than the comparable cost for the lowliest owner-occupier.[14] Similarly for private tenants. On average in 1977 the rent and maintenance costs of tenants in privately furnished accommodation was nearly twice as much as that of local authority tenants, while those of tenants in private unfurnished accommodation was slightly less (*ibid.*). Since privately rented dwellings are on average of lower quality than local authority ones, it is reasonable to infer that the cost of privately renting a house worth £10,000 would have been greater in 1977 than renting it from a local authority. Hence the housing costs for private tenants, too, are likely to be considerably greater than for owner-occupiers.

Since the higher income groups contain a larger proportion of owner-occupiers, and since they also face higher marginal tax rates, the implication of this analysis is that the rich on average face lower money costs than the poor. For the same reasons this will also be true of the costs faced by the higher socio-economic groups relative to those for the lower ones. Hence the *higher* the social group, the *lower* the money cost per unit of housing – a bizarre reversal of the normal standards of justice. Moreover, if each pound spent represents a lesser sacrifice the higher the income, the inequality of costs in terms of that sacrifice will be yet greater than that of money costs.

How far can this situation be attributed to the system of public expenditure on housing? In part, it derives from the tax expenditures that arise through the failure to tax imputed income. If imputed income were taxed then, if all interest rates and rates of return were equal, the annual cost of owner-occupied housing would become independent of the tax rate and the size of the mortgage.[15] In that case owner-occupiers facing high tax rates and/or with a high mortgage (generally, the wealthier ones) would not face lower costs of purchasing a given house than any other owner-occupier. However, the cost for an owner-occupier would almost certainly still be below that of equivalent housing for a council tenant, because any annual increase in the value of the owner-occupier's asset – the house – would partly (or wholly) offset his costs. This remains true, even if capital gains in owner-occupied property were to be taxed.[16] Hence the elimination of all tax expenditures would go some way towards reducing inequalities in housing costs, but it would not eliminate them entirely.

The Distribution of Housing

That inequalities in housing conditions are still a salient feature of British society will come as no surprise to anyone familiar with the squares of Belgravia and the tenements of Bethnal Green or the Cheshire suburbs of Manchester and the slums of Moss Side. But geography and custom mean that in fact very few are familiar with both of the extremes. The view of grey walls, broken windows and cramped backyards from the commuter train is the closest many of the middle class come to housing poverty. Nor do the poor have a better perception of the housing conditions of the rich. They have little occasion to visit wealthy districts and, even if they did, they would find it difficult to penetrate the screen of walls, trees and hedges with which the affluent protect themselves from view.

Hence again it is only measures of housing conditions based on comprehensive surveys which can give a proper picture. But to obtain the appropriate measure, it is necessary to have some idea of what is meant by 'housing', – no easy task, since peoples' houses differ in a wide variety of ways. There are many different dimensions associated with a house, many different factors which affect the well-being of those living in it. These include:

- type (detached, semi-detached or terraced house; high- or low-rise flat, etc.),
- number and size of rooms,
- the provision of amenities (such as inside lavatories, bathrooms and central heating) and their quality,
- location (proximity to public transport, busy roads, parks, industrial areas, etc.).

Any assessment of the distribution of housing therefore requires some estimate of the distribution of as many of these characteristics as possible. No information is available on location, and relatively little on the others; what does exist (mostly from the General Household Survey) is summarised in Table 5.4. The second column shows the percentage of households in each group who live at a density of one or more persons per room. Perhaps surprisingly, the class gradient is not smooth with the bottom group having almost twice the proportion of households living at this density as the top group, but the skilled

Table 5.4   *Housing Conditions by Socio-Economic Group*

All households				Great Britain, 1977
Socio-economic group	One or more persons per room	One or more rooms above bedroom standard	With central heating	Living in detached or semi-detached house
Professionals, employers and managers	5	77	76	69
Intermediate and junior non-manual	7	65	57	49
Skilled manual	15	62	46	48
Semi- and unskilled manual	11	56	34	36

Source: OPCS (1979, p. 34, Table 3.25; p. 35, Table 3.27; p. 39, Table 3.34) and unpublished data from the 1977 GHS.

manual group even more. Precisely why this should be is not clear; it is not a freak of the year, because a similar anomaly appears in every year of the GHS.[17] The third column shows the percentage of all the households in each group with one room or more above the 'bedroom standard', that is, the percentage with one room more than the 'standard' number for households of a given size and composition.[18] This time the gradient is smooth, with the top group having a substantially higher proportion than the bottom group. The fourth and fifth columns give some indication of differences in the quality of housing. Over three-quarters of the top group have central heating, compared with just over a third of the bottom group, and 70 per cent of the top group live in a detached or semi-detached house, compared with over a third of the bottom group.

Breakdowns of the population by annual income show a similar picture. The English House Conditions Survey of 1976 found that over a quarter of those households with incomes below £2,000 p.a. were living in houses defined as in need of rehabilitation, compared with just 6 per cent of those earning over £5,200. Viewed another way, of all the houses described by the survey as in need of rehabilitation, or as lacking basic amenities, nearly half were occupied by households with no one in paid employment and three quarters of the remainder were dependent on low-paid jobs.[19] Townsend's comprehensive survey (1979) found that 'nearly half the population with net income worth of

less than half the mean were found to have inadequate housing
facilities, and over a third to have insufficient indoor playspace for
children, compared with figures of only 3 per cent and 2 per cent
respectively for people with twice or more than twice the mean.
Forty per cent had housing with standard defects compared with
9 per cent' (p. 502). Overall, it appears that, whatever other effects
the system of housing subsidy has had, creating equality in
housing itself is not one of them.

Equality and Policy

An important recent influence on social policy towards housing
has been a concern for equality. Sometimes this is explicit, as in
Crosland's argument that 'the essential requirement, obviously, is
to reduce the gross inequality in *physical* housing conditions'
(1974, p. 125, emphasis in original). More often, it appears in the
form of a concern for 'fairness'. Thus the Conservative
government's White Paper of 1971, significantly entitled *Fair
Deal for Housing*, included as two of its three principal objectives
'a fairer choice between owning a home and renting one' and
'fairness between one citizen and another in giving and receiving
help towards housing costs' (p. 1). Similar references appear in
the subsequent Labour government's Green Paper *Housing Policy*
(1977) (see, for instance, p. 41). Although not explicitly stated in
terms of equality, objectives such as these may be readily
interpreted as referring to some of the various conceptions of
equality outlined in Chapter 2. For there to be fairness of choice
between owning a home and renting one, it would seem essential
that there be *equality of costs* between tenures. Fairness in giving
and receiving help towards housing costs could also be
interpreted in terms of equality of costs, but it is more likely to
imply either the objective of *equality of public expenditure* or that
of *equality of final income*.

Whichever interpretation is chosen, the evidence suggests that
the objectives have not been achieved. There exist substantial
inequalities of public expenditure, with owner-occupiers
receiving more than private or public tenants and the better off
receiving more than the less well off. The system thus also
promotes inequality in final income. Moreover, the subsidy
system is in large part responsible for the existence of large

inequalities in costs between owner-occupiers and tenants and between owner-occupiers themselves.

The principal item creating the pro-rich inequality in public expenditure is the expenditure that arises from the operation of the tax system. The exemptions from tax of housing 'income' and capital gains from owner-occupied dwellings result in a considerable subsidy to all owner-occupiers, one that, moreover, favours the wealthier owner-occupiers. Partly because of this and partly because owner-occupation itself is more prevalent among the higher income groups, the richest quarter of the population receives over six times as much subsidy per household from this source as the poorest fifth. On the other hand, with the exception of improvement grants, direct public expenditure favours the less well off, with the poorest group in the population receiving on average about three times as much expenditure on general subsidies to council tenants and rent rebates as the richest group. However, the pro-poor distribution of direct expenditures is not sufficient to offset the pro-rich distribution of tax expenditures. The net result is that the richest group receives nearly twice as much public subsidy per household as the poorest group.

Tax expenditures are also one of the major reasons why there exist disparities in costs (even for similar housing) between income and tenure groups. These are considerable. Per 'unit' of housing, both private and council tenants pay more than most owner-occupiers, and poorer owner-occupiers pay more than richer ones. Indeed some wealthy owner-occupiers actually face negative costs of housing; in other words, they are being paid to live in their houses.

From this, it would appear that an obvious policy change that would promote greater equality, at least of public expenditure and costs, would be the reduction (or even elimination) of tax expenditures, particularly if any consequent increase in tax revenue was used to increase the incomes of the poor. If, for instance, the taxation of capital gains in owner-occupied housing were introduced and the taxation of imputed income was *re*-introduced, then (so long as no additional loopholes or other tax avoidance devices were included) there is little doubt that this would have a considerable impact on the distribution of public expenditure, costs and final income. Tax expenditures would be eliminated, leaving improvement grants as the only part of the system that favoured the better off. Since they are small relative to the other subsidies the result would be an aggregate distribution of public expenditure that was unambiguously pro-poor, a substantial reduction in inequalities in housing costs, and greater equality in final incomes.

But there are a number of possible objections. First, it could be argued that there are practical problems in the valuation of imputed income, although the fact that imputed income is taxed in most other EEC countries suggests that these problems are not insuperable. Second, there may be short-term redistributive consequences, which might be undesirable. For instance, the introduction of a tax on imputed income might prove a considerable burden on an old-age pensioner couple who had paid off their mortgage. But the revenue raised by the tax changes could be used to offset this or any other undesirable redistributive consequences. Third, it is often argued that it would be unfair to tax owner-occupiers on the capital gains they have made on their houses, since any new home they move into will also have risen in price. But this is true of all sales of capital assets. Should shareholders be exempt from tax on the capital gains they make from selling shares on the grounds that any more they wish to buy may also have risen in price? Moreover, there is evidence to show that, on average, those who move use some of their capital gain to finance personal consumption (see Lansley, 1979, pp. 106–7). On balance therefore these seem to be desirable reforms.

An alternative proposal is the elimination of mortgage interest tax relief. This would reduce the tax expenditures incident upon owner-occupiers and hence reduce inequality in the distribution of public expenditure. Unlike the other tax changes, it would not eliminate these expenditures (if the latter are defined as the absence of taxation on capital gains and imputed income), but it might be more practical and would have fewer undesirable short-term redistributive consequences. Thus it would reduce the administrative burden on the Inland Revenue, and would increase the tax burden on those most able to bear it – mortgaged owner-occupiers. Moreover, if inflation continues the relief could be phased out fairly painlessly, simply by keeping the present £25,000 limit constant. This therefore might be a more politically acceptable tax change than the others.

Changes in direct expenditure policies that would affect inequality include reducing council house rents by increasing the general subsidy, raising the income level for eligibility for rent rebates and allowances and the selling of council houses. An increase in the general subsidy would reduce the average level of (unrebated) council rents, and thereby reinforce the pro-poor nature of this item of public expenditure. It would also reduce inequality in costs between council tenants and owner-occupiers (though it would increase them between council and private tenants). However, since the subsidy benefits only council tenants such a move would not be as effective in promoting all three types of equality as raising the eligibility level for rent rebates and allowances – at least in principle. Unfortunately, the reality may differ from the principle, due to that seemingly insoluble problem of means-tested benefits, the reluctance of many individuals to take them up. Most sales of council houses are at reduced prices to existing tenants, implying a one-off capital gain to them. This would create greater equality in public expenditure during the year in which they occurred, but the effect on distribution in subsequent years is difficult to forecast, since the reduction in direct expenditure incident upon the households concerned would be wholly or partly offset by an increase in tax expenditures due to their new status as owner-occupiers. However, it is probably safe to predict that there would be greater equality of costs.

Finally, would any of these changes have a significant impact on the distribution of housing itself? It seems unlikely, unless they were carried out on a massive scale. Even if money costs per unit of housing were equalised for all groups (and none of the proposed changes are likely to achieve that) differences in the sacrifice represented by these costs would remain, and so long as these continue, inequality in housing conditions will persist. The fundamental reason why the better off have better housing conditions is because they are better off, and there is not a great deal that housing policy of whatever kind can do about that. As the nineteenth century social reformer, Dr John Simon, said (quoted in Bruce, 1973, p. 82):

> Question, how the house-accommodation of the poor labouring classes may be rendered such as humane persons would wish it to be, is therefore necessarily in great part question, how far poverty can be turned into non-poverty, how far the poor can be made less poor.

Notes to Chapter 5

1   Appendix B, Table B.1.

2   The tax allowance for interest on loans for the purchase and improvement of owner-occupied property, the exemption of that property from capital gains tax and the exemptions and reduced rates of stamp duty also associated with owner-occupied property have been estimated by the Board of Inland Revenue as costing £2,885 million in 1978–9 (1979, Table 1.10, pp. 15–17).

3   Other useful discussions of some of the topics treated include Grey, Hepworth and Odling-Smee (1978), Lansley (1979, Ch. 5), Robinson (1979, Ch. 9) and Whitehead (1980).

4   Estimates of the distribution of public housing expenditures are also included in the aggregate estimates of the distribution of taxes and benefits in the UK listed in Appendix A (p. 155); but as with those for health care and education, they were generally allocated simply by assumption.

5   That is, there are no 'externalities' or 'shifting'. There is further discussion of the shifting issue in the main text, pp. 93–4; for a wider treatment of the problem, together with a discussion of the externality issue and explanation of the terms, see Appendix A.

6   Townsend (1979, pp. 976–9) also makes accounting-cost estimates of the distribution of general subsidies; but these are cruder than those described here (he simply allocates to each local authority household the average general subsidy for that local authority).

7   Calculated from Department of Employment (1979, Table 6, pp. 30–1).

8   The percentage take-up rate has been estimated at 55 to 60 per cent for 1977 and 1978 (Department of the Environment, 1980, p. 147, Table 121(a)).

9   Willis and Hardwick (1978) consider both the absence of a tax on imputed income *and* the mortgage interest deduction to be tax expenditures, arguing (p. 47) that non-business interest payments are no longer allowable against tax liability.

10 Hughes's estimates differ from Robinson's in that he compares the existing tax system with one where (1) the capital gains tax rate is the same as the income tax rate and (2) the tax system is indexed for inflation. But, for the purpose of computing *housing* tax expenditures, it seems preferable to compare the present system with one that would be neutral with respect to those features of the present system that are specific to housing. The tax expenditures which arise due to the capital gains tax rate not being equal to the income tax rate and the 'over'-taxation due to the absence of indexation are both much wider problems (affecting a broader class of taxpayer), and hence arguably should not be taken on board in a study concerned only with housing subsidies.

11 Hughes did a more systematic analysis of the relationship between aggregate public expenditure and income group, and found that, except for the lowest and the two highest groups, the magnitude of the housing subsidy was essentially independent of income. His estimates have the merit of including the tax subsidy to private tenants; unfortunately, they are also affected by the problem mentioned in the preceding note.

12 The issue is also discussed in Townsend (1979, pp. 505–14).
13 Suppose V is the market value of a dwelling and π is the rate of increase in the value of that dwelling. Let M be the value of any mortgage debt outstanding, r the rate of interest on the mortgage, R the (before-tax) rate of return on alternative investment, K the cost of maintenance and t the income tax rate. Then the cost of housing services, C, is given by:

$$C = R(1 - t) (V - M) + r (1 - t)M - \pi \ V + K.$$

14 For instance, an owner-occupier of a £10,000 house with no mortgage and facing a 30 per cent tax rate would, under the assumptions of Table 5.3, have a total housing cost of £370.
15 If imputed income is taxed then the cost of housing (see note 13) becomes:

$$C = R(1 - t) (V - M) + r (1 - t)M - \pi \ V + K + tR^*V$$

when R^* is the rate of return on housing. If $R^* = r = R$ (that is, if all rates of return and interest rates are equal) then $C = RV - \pi \ V + K$ and the cost is independent of the tax rate and the mortgage.
16 If tenants were charged an amount equal to the return on housing, and if all rates of return were equal, then their cost would be RV (see note 15). This would be greater than the cost for owner-occupiers, even if capital gains were taxed, for this cost would be $RV - (1 - t_c) \pi \ V + K$, where t_c is the capital gains tax rate.
17 In a personal communication, Tony Atkinson has suggested that it may reflect the higher degree of owner-occupation among the skilled manual group than among the semi- and unskilled manual group.
18 The standard number is determined by allocating one bedroom each to a married couple, any single person 21 and over, any pair of children aged 10–20 of the same sex, and each pair of children under 10. Any unpaired person aged 10–20 is paired if possible with a child under 10 of the same sex, or, if that is not possible, is given a separate bedroom, as is any unpaired child under 10. See OPCS (1980, p. 163).
19 Department of the Environment (1979, p. 5 and p. 36, Table D.2.12).

CHAPTER 6

Transport

Though transport services are used by people of all ages and incomes, and subsidies benefit all who use them, the test of whether a subsidy will help towards a fairer distribution of income is one way in which its value can be judged.
Transport Policy, Cmnd 6836

The provision of adequate means of transport for its citizens has long been regarded as a legitimate function of the state. Most Western governments subsidise both private and public transport, private transport through, for instance, the provision of highways free of direct charge, and public transport through direct grants to operators. Currently in Britain expenditure on transport makes up approximately 4 per cent of total public expenditure, half of which goes on roads and about a fifth each on subsidies to British Rail and to bus, underground and ferry services.[1] British Rail gets about half of its total revenue from government sources, while the London Underground and bus and coach operators both receive approximately a fifth.[2]

Such expenditures have often been justified, at least in part, on distributional grounds. Hence it is important to establish their actual distributional impact, in so far as that is possible. The first section of this chapter discusses the evidence concerning the distribution of public expenditure on public transport (principally rail and bus services), while the second considers that for private transport (principally the car). The third examines briefly the distribution of what could be regarded as the 'outcome' of such expenditure, that is, travel itself. The final section summarises the evidence concerning distribution, relates it to the objectives of equality and discusses the ways in which one might be brought more in line with the other.

The Distribution of Public Expenditure on Public Transport

A breakdown of public expenditure on public transport in Great Britain for 1978–9 is given in Figure 6.1 The total amounted to over £1,100 million, of which nearly half went to British Rail and most of the rest to bus and underground operators. Over 70 per cent of grants to British Rail are designed to cover unremunerative passenger services; the remainder represents grants to assist with the pension fund, the provision of level crossings and so on. The London Underground receives grants from the Greater London Council to cover its operating deficits and also for capital expenditure. Bus and coach operators receive grants (generally from local authorities) to cover operating and capital deficits. They also receive grants to help with the purchase

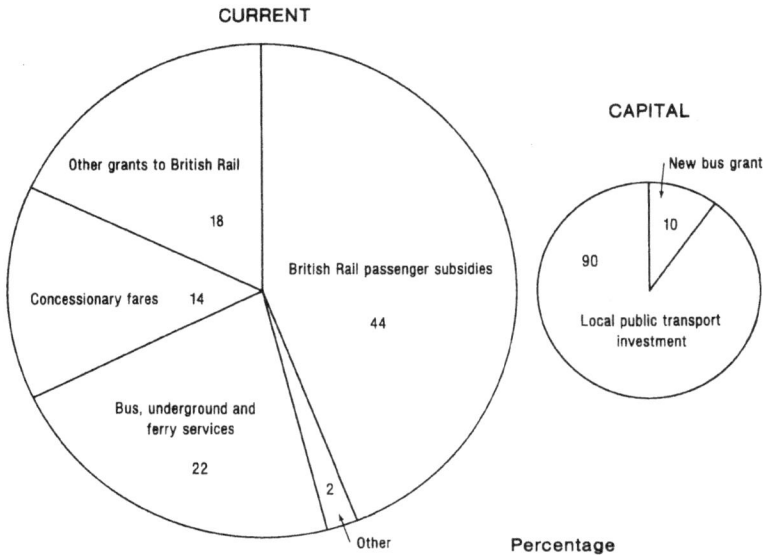

CURRENT

CAPITAL

Other grants to British Rail

18

Concessionary fares   14

British Rail passenger subsidies

44

Bus, underground and ferry services

22

2

Other

New bus grant

10

90

Local public transport investment

Percentage

Figure 6.1   Public expenditure on public transport by category, Great Britain 1978–9.
Source: Appendix B, Table B1.

of new buses, and their passengers benefit from grants for concessionary fare schemes.

Three important sources of subsidy are omitted from Figure 6.1. Several times over the past decade British Rail and London Transport have had their capital debts written off by the central government, a subsidy that between 1969 and 1975 amounted to £1,717 million.[3] Bus operators receive a rebate on fuel tax (a form of tax expenditure); in 1978 this cost £59 million.[4] Also, bus operators do not have to pay directly for the costs arising from their use of the road network, costs that were estimated for 1975–6 as £65 million and for 1980–1 as £75 million.[5]

With one exception, to be discussed shortly, there are no direct estimates of the distribution of public expenditure on public transport between different social groups for the UK. Most researchers have based their work on the distribution of *private* expenditure on public transport as revealed by, for instance, the Family Expenditure Survey (FES),[6] a distribution which is therefore assumed accurately to reflect the distribution of public subsidy. The implications of this assumption will be discussed in a moment; in the mean time, the distribution of private expenditure by income group from the 1978 FES is given in the third and fourth columns of Table 6.1.

For anyone who believes public transport to be a preserve of the poor, the results are astonishing. The richest fifth of the population spends nearly *ten times* as much on rail fares (British Rail and the London Underground) as the poorest fifth. Put another way, over half of rail passenger revenue from private sources comes from the top fifth of the income distribution compared with just 4 per cent from the bottom fifth.[7] Perhaps yet more surprisingly, expenditure on bus and coach fares shows a similar pattern, albeit one in which the inequality is not so marked. The richest group spends nearly four times as much per household on bus and coach fares as the poorest; they contribute over a third of all bus company revenues from private sources compared with less than 7 per cent from the poorest group.

Part of the explanation for this inequality lies in the differences in household sizes between the income groups. One study (Department of the Environment, 1976, Vol. 2, Paper 2) attempted to correct for these differences. Household incomes were 'adjusted', via an (unspecified) weighting procedure according to their size, with larger households having their

Table 6.1   *Household Expenditure on Transport by Income Group*

All households				*United Kingdom, 1978*
Income[a] group (p.a.)	*Percentage of population*	*Weekly expenditure per household: percentage of mean*		
		Rail fares	*Bus and coach fares*	*Motoring[b]*
£7,800 or more	21.8	244	145	204
£5,720–£7,799	19.7	104	123	227
£4,160–£5,719	18.1	69	102	98
£2,080–£4,159	22.8	40	82	47
Less than £2,080	17.5	25	40	12
Mean (= 100) (£)	—	0.52	0.88	8.66

[a] Gross income.

[b] Net purchases of motor vehicles, spares and accessories, plus expenditure on the maintenance and running of motor vehicles.

Source: Calculated from Department of Employment (1979, Table 6, pp. 36–7; Table 1, p. 22).

income reduced relative to smaller ones. The households were then grouped into adjusted income groups, and their expenditure on public transport divided up accordingly. Some results are shown in Table 6.2. Comparison with Table 6.1 reveals that the adjustment for household size makes little difference as far as rail travel is concerned, with the gap between top and bottom narrowing only slightly. Unfortunately, the figures for bus travel in Table 6.2 are not directly comparable to those in Table 6.1 since the latter includes coach travel while the former does not. However, it does appear that, when household size is taken into account, the gradient for bus travel excluding coaches is not unambiguously pro-rich; in particular, the highest income group has an average expenditure below that of all groups except the lowest.

Little work has been done on the distribution of household expenditure by occupational groups. Results from the one study that has investigated this are shown in Table 6.3. The data are again from the Family Expenditure Survey; hence the occupational groups are those used by the survey, which unfortunately do not correspond directly to the classifications used elsewhere in this book. None the less, they give an

Table 6.2   *Household Expenditure on Public Transport by Adjusted Income Group*

All households		Great Britain, 1972–3
Adjusted income group[a]	*Weekly expenditure per household: percentage of mean*[b]	
	Rail fares	Bus fares
Top 20 %	240	90
Next 20 %	115	130
Middle 20 %	70	110
Next 20 %	45	95
Bottom 20 %	30	75

[a] Household gross income, adjusted for differences in household size.
[b] Mean not available from source table.
Source: Calculated from Department of the Environment (1976, Vol. 2, Paper 2, p. 33, Table 1, Case 2 and p. 41, Table 9).

Table 6.3   *Household Expenditure on Public Transport by Occupational Group*

All households[a]		United Kingdom, 1973
Occupational group	*Expenditure per household (£ per week)* [b]	
	Rail fares	Bus and coach fares
Professional, technical and administrative	0.63	0.40
Teacher, clerical and shop assistant	0.48	0.49
Manual	0.16	0.70

[a] Households headed by the self-employed, retired or unemployed are omitted.
[b] Mean not available in source table.
Source: Grey (1975, p. 124, Table 6.7).

indication. The top group – which very roughly corresponds to the top socio-economic group (professionals, employers and managers) – has about four times the expenditure on rail fares of the bottom group (corresponding to the skilled, semi- and unskilled manual workers' socio-economic groups); but they have considerably *less* average expenditure on bus fares. Overall, while those at the higher end of the social and economic scale spend considerably more than those at the bottom on rail travel, it seems as though the difference is not nearly so pronounced for bus travel and indeed may even be reversed.

That the lower socio-economic groups do use bus services more than the higher ones is borne out by evidence from the National Travel Survey, which shows that the number of journeys per person made per week by bus on average in unskilled manual workers' households is over three times as many as that by those in professional households.[8] Number of journeys is not a perfect indicator of use, since journey lengths vary; none the less, the evidence is indicative of a pattern of distribution that favours the lowest groups.

Before the relationship between the distribution of household expenditure and that of public expenditure is discussed, the one study that provides estimates of the latter should be mentioned. These are estimates of the rail subsidy which have recently been included by the Central Statistical Office in its annual estimates of the incidence of taxes and public expenditure. Unfortunately, these give little more information than the household expenditure distribution discussed already; for they are derived directly from those distributions. More specifically, the average subsidy per household for each income group is taken as equal to a fixed proportion of the average household's private expenditure on rail travel. The proportion is the same for all income groups and corresponds roughly to the proportion of total public subsidy to total British Rail receipts from non-government sources. Some recent results are given in Appendix B, Table B.3; not surprisingly, given their derivation, they too show a pro-rich distribution.

Now it is necessary to examine the validity of the assumption that the distribution of household expenditure on public transport matches that of the relevant public expenditure. This will be correct if two conditions hold: first, the price of each 'unit' of transport faced by each user is the same; second, that the amount of public expenditure associated with each unit is the same. The role of these last two conditions is demonstrated algebraically in a note[9] but the point can be made with a simple example. Suppose one group of individuals faced lower prices for public transport than another group because, for one reason or another, the trips by the first group were being more heavily subsidised from public funds (thus neither of the conditions is being met). Then because the price is lower to the first group, their private expenditure will also be lower; but, since their transport is being more heavily subsidised, their share of public expenditure will be higher. In other words, the distribution of public expenditure would be the exact *opposite* of the distribution of private expenditure.

Although in practice these conditions are not fulfilled, it is unlikely that the effect of this is to reverse the inequality, as in the example, or even substantially to diminish it. In recent years there has been a spread of concessionary schemes lowering the price of public transport to certain groups in society. In particular, old age pensioners now travel free on London buses; they get reduced fares in other cities and also benefit from substantial reductions in rail and tube fares. Since they constitute a large proportion of the poor, it could be argued that the effect of these concessions must be to reduce the amount of the latter's private expenditure relative to use, and hence – if private expenditure is being used as a proxy for public expenditure – to underestimate their share of public subsidy. But this would only be true if each unit of use by these groups involved public subsidy to the same extent as that of other travellers. In fact, the majority of these schemes only apply in off-peak periods, times when, for most forms of public transport, the cost of carrying an extra passenger is very low, if not zero. Hence the public expenditure attributable to passengers using the concessionary schemes is virtually negligible; and the existence of such schemes is not therefore likely to have a serious effect on the conclusion that the distribution of subsidy is basically pro-rich.

Moreover, there is a group concentrated in the higher income groups who also benefit from price reductions but whose trips actually cost more per unit than those of other travellers: commuters.[10] Commuter services are expensive to run, since the heavy morning and evening peaks need rolling stock and a complex infra-structure which are under-used at other times. As a result, contrary to popular belief, they are substantial loss makers. For instance, it can be estimated that the London and South-East commuter service alone contributes to over a third of British Rail's losses on passenger services.[11] The implication of this is that the higher income groups' share of public expenditure is actually larger than their share of private expenditure would indicate, and hence that the inequality in the former is actually greater than in the latter.

Against this it could be argued that commuters are not necessarily the principal beneficiaries from the subsidies to commuting; for it is possible that the subsidies are 'capitalised' in the prices of houses that commuters buy. Thus houses in close proximity to a railway or underground station may be more expensive than similar housing elsewhere. But, as with the similar argument for tax expenditures on housing (above, pp. 93–4), the force of this argument will depend on the reference point chosen. For instance, it could be just as plausibly maintained that commuters do benefit from the subsidies, since if the latter were removed tomorrow the value of their assets would fall. None the less, the fact that the eventual incidence of a particular subsidy may not be identical with the users of the subsidised service should be borne in mind.

Overall, it is likely that the distribution of private expenditure is not too inaccurate an indicator of the distribution of public expenditure and hence that the latter, like the former, is quite unequal – particularly for rail travel.

The Distribution of Public Expenditure on Private Transport

The principal form of private transport is the car, and it is this that will be dealt with in this section. Public expenditure on private travel by car in Britain takes two forms: direct public expenditure through the provision of roads at no direct charge for use, and tax expenditures associated with the provision of company cars.

First, in the case of direct expenditures, as with public transport, there have been no studies of the distribution of public expenditure as such. It is therefore necessary to rely on evidence concerning the distribution of private expenditure.[12] That from the 1978 FES is summarised in the fourth column of Table 6.1 whence it is apparent that, not surprisingly, the distribution is quite unequal. Interestingly, the gradient is not smooth, with the richest fifth of the income distribution spending less on private motoring than the next richest. This almost certainly arises because a substantial portion of private motoring by the wealthier groups is actually paid for by employers (through the provision of the 'company car'); hence the inequality in the private use of the road system is probably even greater than these figures indicate.

That a similar pattern exists for socio-economic groups can be inferred from the evidence of the General Household Survey on car ownership, summarised in Figure 6.2, which shows that the proportion of the top group which owns a car is nearly three times that of the bottom group (although again it should be

All Households   Great Britain, 1978

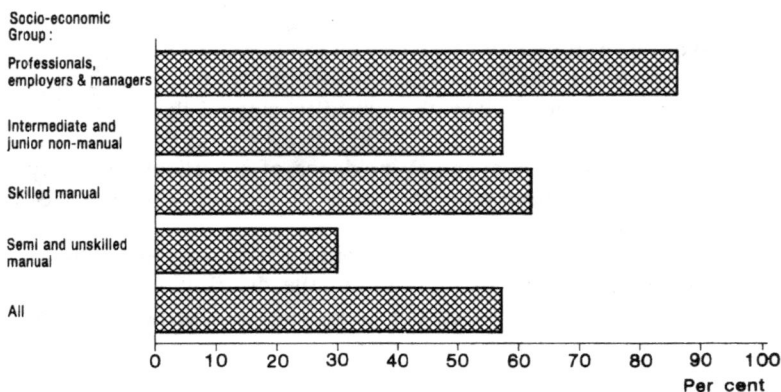

Figure 6.2   Car ownership by socio-economic group.
        Source: OPCS (1980, p. 45, Table 3.31. London: HMSO, 1979).

observed that the gradient is not smooth). Further support comes
from evidence provided by the National Travel Survey showing
that journeys by private car per person in professional,
employers' and managers' households is approximately three
times that per person in those of semi- and unskilled manual
workers.[13] Hence it is reasonable to conclude that the distribution
of public expenditure on roads favours the higher social groups,
whether the latter are defined in terms of income or occupation.

This conclusion could be challenged on the grounds that it
ignores the taxes paid by motorists. These include vehicle excise
duties, car tax (purchase tax on new cars), taxes on petrol and
VAT – taxes which could be viewed as a kind of 'charge' for the
use of the road system and which, for private cars at least, have
been estimated as generating more revenue annually than the
public road costs associated with private motoring.[14] On this
interpretation, the road system as a whole constitutes not an item
of public expenditure but one of public revenue, contributing
more to the public budget than it takes out.

This argument would be more persuasive if the revenue from
such taxes was earmarked for expenditure on roads. As it is,
however, these revenues go into the general pool of taxation, and
decisions concerning the rate at which they are levied on private

motorists appear to be based more on the state of aggregate demand in the economy than on the needs of the nation's road system. Similarly, decisions concerning public expenditure on roads are little affected by considerations of the revenue being generated by these taxes. On balance, therefore, it seems preferable to view them as part of the taxation system with redistributive consequences separate from those due to the public expenditure system.

A part of the taxation system which corresponds more directly to public expenditure is the income tax provisions for company cars. The value of a car provided to an employee by his or her employer is taxed under the income tax system via a procedure that is generally thought to lead to less tax being paid than would be the case if the employee had received the equivalent in cash. More specifically, those under a certain earnings level (£7,500 in 1978) escape tax on a company car altogether, even if the car is provided for mainly private use, while those with earnings above that level have to add a sum on to their taxable income which 'it is clear ... does not represent the full value of private usage' (Royal Commission on the Distribution of Income and Wealth, 1979, p. 132). If this is correct – and there is some reason for doubt[15] – since the provision of company cars for private use is by and large an executive perk, it seems that this too is another area of public expenditure which favours the better off.

The Distribution of Travel

The distribution of travel itself, as revealed in the National Travel Survey, is shown in Tables 6.4 (by income group) and 6.5 (by socio-economic group). Two indicators of the amount of travel undertaken are given: the mileage travelled and the number of journeys undertaken. The top SEGs do over twice as much mileage per person per week as the bottom two SEGs, although only a quarter as many more journeys. The distribution by income group shows a similar pattern, with each person in the top quarter of the population doing about a third more journeys on average than anyone in the bottom fifth, but in the process covering nearly three times as many miles. The survey also gives the mileage distributions broken down by journey purpose (travel to and from work, holidays, shopping, etc.); no matter what the

Table 6.4   *Travel by Income Group*

All persons			*Great Britain 1975–6*
Income group[a] *(p.a.)*	*Percentage of population*	*Journeys per person per week: percentage of mean*	*Mileage per person: percentage of mean*
£5,000 or more	27.7	117	140
£4,000–£4,999	16.4	109	115
£3,000–£3,999	17.5	101	97
£2,000–£2,999	18.0	95	81
Less than £2,000	20.4	74	53
Mean	—	18.0	90.2

[a] Gross income.

Source: Calculated from Department of Transport (1979a, p. 53, Table 4.9 and p. 54, Table 4.10).

Table 6.5   *Travel by Socio-Economic Group*

All persons		*Great Britain 1975–6*
Socio-economic group[a]	*Journeys per person per week: percentage of mean*	*Mileage per person per week: percentage of mean*
Professionals, employers and managers	112	145
Intermediate and junior non-manual	107	115
Skilled manual	97	86
Semi- and unskilled manual	88	66
Mean	18.2	92.8

[a] About 2 per cent of the sample population was unclassified.

Source: Calculated from Department of Transport (1979a, p. 52, Table 4.7 and p. 53, Table 4.8).

purpose, the higher social groups (both SEGs and income) do more on average than the lower groups.

Equality and Policy

Subsidies for public transport have been justified in a number of ways. Prominent among them has been the desire to improve the distribution of resources. Alexander Grey, sometime head of the Public Transport Division of the Greater London Council, in his book on urban transport produced a list of 'illustrative aims' for transport policy, the first of which was 'to redistribute income from rich to poor people' (Grey, 1975, p. 21). A recent White Paper on transport policy argued that 'the test of whether a subsidy will help towards a fairer distribution of income is one way in which its value can be judged' (*Transport Policy*, 1977, p. 12); while the House of Commons Select Committee on Nationalised Industries has described 'redistribution via public spending' as the 'usual implicit aim' of public transport subsidies (Select Committee, 1977, p. lxxxvii).

In terms of the objectives specified in Chapter 2, these statements all seem to imply that a major aim of transport subsidies is to promote greater *equality of final income*. That is, public expenditure on transport should benefit the poor more than the rich. If this is indeed one of the objectives of transport policy, it is clear that, in this respect at least, it has failed. On average, the subsidy for rail travel by the highest income groups is nearly ten times that of the lowest, while that on private transport (through the provision of roads) is seventeen times. The distribution of public expenditure on bus travel is less clear. It appears to benefit more those higher up the social scale in terms of income, but those lower down in terms of occupation. All in all, however, it seems reasonable to assert that public expenditures on transport have not promoted greater equality in final income.

Although the other equality objectives specified in Chapter 2 – equality of public expenditure, of use, of cost and of outcome – do not figure conspicuously in government statements concerning policy aims, it is worth noting that they have not been achieved either. As we have seen, there exists substantial inequality in public expenditure, at least in the case of rail and private transport, which in turn reflects a substantial inequality in use. The fare concessions on public transport to, particularly, old age pensioners and commuters contribute to inequalities in the money costs of transport faced by different social groups. And while the concessions to old age pensioners, who are primarily on low incomes, may go some way towards creating equality in terms of the actual sacrifices involved, those to commuters, with generally higher incomes, create greater inequality in such sacrifices.

Finally, substantial inequalities of outcome persist, whether measured in terms of number of journeys or mileage travelled, with, for instance, those in the top income and socio-economic groups travelling over twice as far on average as the bottom groups.

What are the prospects for reform? It is difficult to imagine any change which preserves or increases the present levels of subsidies that would substantially reduce inequality. Indeed, many of those suggested (such as tax allowances for commuters' travelling expenses) would simply make matters worse. Rather, if the aim is to promote equality in almost any sense of the term, the most obvious policy reform is to reduce, in so far as it is possible, the public subsidisation of transport. All public transport operators could be required to cover their costs, and peak-hour road-pricing schemes could be introduced so as to relate more exactly the costs road users impose on the rest of society to the price they pay. Any money saved, or revenue raised, could be used to promote equality in a more direct fashion, through, for instance, direct cash subsidies to the poor.

Desirable though such reforms might be from an egalitarian point of view, there is little doubt they would encounter considerable opposition. For instance, the requirement that public transport operators should cover their costs could be criticised on at least five counts, all concerned with the promotion of allocative efficiency. First, public transport systems are supposed to confer 'external benefits', that is, benefits to third parties not directly using the system. In particular, the existence of a rail commuter network reduces peak-hour congestion on roads, thus enabling road commuters to complete their journey in a shorter time. Second, many forms of public transport have high fixed costs (for instance, railways have high costs of installation and maintenance of track), and a price set to cover these costs may not be that which would maximise the net gain to society. In these circumstances, the community may find it worthwhile to allow the industry to price below average cost and to meet the inevitable deficit out of public funds. A third efficiency consideration is that there may be what economists have termed 'option demand' for public transport, that is, people may be prepared to pay in order to keep a public transport system in existence just in case they might need it – even if that eventuality never actually arises. Fourth, public transport is often thought to be more economical than private transport in energy use; and, fifth, public transport in rural areas is often justified on the grounds that it contributes favourably towards maintaining economic activity in those areas.

There is not the space here to examine these arguments in detail. But it is worth noting that some are less persuasive than others. For instance, the 'external benefits' of public transport only arise because the costs of road travel are also subsidised. Motorists do not have to pay directly for the costs they inflict on others through traffic congestion; hence, other things being equal, they will tend to overuse highway facilities, particularly at peak hours. The sensible solution to this problem is not additionally to subsidise public transport; rather it is to introduce some form of peak-hour road-pricing or some other form of traffic control. As the White Paper on transport policy says: 'It is sometimes argued that subsidies should be paid to public transport to attract travellers out of cars and so reduce congestion on the roads. But this can be a valid reason only where road congestion is a severe problem and where it would cost more to tackle it directly by traffic management or parking controls. The evidence is that there are few places where these conditions are met, and that subsidies paid for this reason are, on the whole, misplaced' (*Transport Policy*, 1977, p. 12). Also, the argument that public transport is more economical in energy use seems to be more of an argument for the proper pricing of all kinds of transport, rather than for subsidising one kind in particular. If road transport was properly priced, and if both private and public transport had to cover their costs, then, everything else being equal, if public transport really had lower energy costs its prices would be lower. And, if its prices were lower, it would be used more and hence energy would be saved.

Many objections could also be raised to the proposal for some form of road-pricing scheme. However, a Ministry of Transport report (1964) found the idea both practical and attractive. A study by the Greater London Council, evaluating a 'supplementary licensing scheme' which would charge all cars entering central London on weekdays concluded that 'in terms of revenue raised and of social cost-benefit, London would gain from a scheme of supplementary licensing. In wider terms, despite some social problems, the broad social and environmental effects would outweigh the disadvantages and the quality of life in London could be expected to improve' (Greater London Council, 1974,

p. 8). Indeed, a similar system is actually in operation in Singapore, and has yielded impressive results in terms of reducing traffic flow and raising the use of public transport (usefully summarised in Anderson *et al.*, 1977, pp. 75–80).

A final objection to the proposal that public subsidisation of transport should be reduced is not concerned either with efficiency or practicality. Rather, it is a form of what was termed in Chapter 2, a 'minimum standards' objective; in the words of the Select Committee of the House of Commons 'to provide an acceptable minimum level of mobility for all members of society ... irrespective of income level or car ownership' (1977, pp. lxxxi–ii). Public subsidies which lead to reduced fares increase the opportunities for the less well off to travel, and hence do move some way towards that objective. This undoubtedly reflects a gain in terms of social justice, but against this gain has to be set the considerable loss, again in terms of social justice, due to the transfer of resources to the better off. An alternative strategy, that would have a similar gain but none of the loss, would be to use the money from a subsidisation of transport instead to raise the incomes of the less well off. Since the bulk of the existing subsidy goes to the better off, the consequent increase in the money income of the poor is likely to be greater than the fall in the value of that income due to the rise in transport costs; hence their travel opportunities would be enhanced (along with all their other opportunities), while those of the better off would be reduced. Both elements of social justice – equality and the attainment of 'minimum levels of mobility' – would thereby be served.

On balance, therefore, it seems as though both equality, however defined, and minimum standards would be achieved by a switch from the public subsidisation of transport to a subsidisation of low incomes. It is very difficult to support continued public subsidy of transport on egalitarian grounds; such expenditure can be justified, if at all, only by reference to the promotion of social and economic efficiency.

Notes to Chapter 6

1   Appendix B, Table B.2.
2, 3, 4   Department of Transport (1979b, p. 2, Table 2, p. 3, Table 3).
5   Department of the Environment (1976, Vol. 2, p. 112); *Hansard,* 28

March 1980, cols 725–6. It is possible to argue that the taxes on bus operators are a kind of 'charge' they pay for the use of the road network, and hence should be offset against their total subsidy; in 1978 these amounted to £89 million, gross of the fuel tax rebate (Department of Transport, 1979b, p. 2, Table 2). As with the similar claim for private motoring (see main text, pp. 114) this argument would be more persuasive if this revenue was actually earmarked for the provision of roads for bus operators.

6 See, for example, Grey (1975, Ch. 6), Pryke and Dodgson (1975, Ch. 9) and Le Grand (1978). Another study (Department of the Environment, 1976, Vol. 2, Paper 2) used the 1972–3 National Travel Survey as the basis for its estimates.

7 This information is not shown directly in Table 6.1, but can be calculated from it.

8 Department of Transport (1979a, p. 52, Table 4.7).

9 The conditions are sufficient, but not necessary. The necessary condition is that the ratio of the prices for each unit used by any two users equals the ratio of the public expenditures for each unit. This can be seen as follows. Let a unit of use be a passenger-kilometre: one kilometre travelled by one passenger. Let p_i and p_j be the prices of a passenger-kilometre to the ith and j^{th} groups, respectively; let n_i and n_j be the number of passenger-kilometres each group travels; and let s_i and s_j be the public expenditure per passenger-kilometre for each group. Then the ratio of private expenditure by one group to that by the other is R_p, where

$$R_p = \frac{p_i \, n_i}{p_j \, n_j}.$$

The ratio of total public expenditure incident upon each group is R_s, where

$$R_s = \frac{s_i \, n_i}{s_j \, n_j}.$$

Then R_p will equal R_s if $p_i/p_j = s_i/s_j$. This condition will of course hold if $p_i = p_j$ and $s_i = s_j$: the two conditions specified in the text.

It should also be noted that a further condition is also necessary, which is that users should be the sole beneficiaries of public expenditure on public transport. In other words, it is necessary to assume there are no 'externalities' or 'shifting'. For an explanation of these terms, and a discussion of the problems involved, see Appendix A. The shifting problem with respect to public transport subsidies to commuters is discussed in the main text, pp. 112–13.

10 For evidence that rail commuters tend to be in the higher income groups, see Department of Transport (1979a, p. 74, Tables 5.8 and 5.9).

11 Estimated from Department of the Environment (1976, Vol. 1, p. 51–2).

12 The only other studies that have allocated public expenditures on roads are Barna (1945), who allocated them in proportion to the taxes falling on motoring, and Cartter (1955), who allocated them according to estimates of his own concerning private expenditure on motoring.

13 Department of Transport (1979a, p. 52, Table 4.7).

14 In 1976–7, the combined revenues from vehicle excise duties, fuel tax, the extra VAT on petrol and car tax from non-business cars were estimated as twice the 'road track costs' attributable to these vehicles (Department of the Environment, 1976, Vol. 2, p. 112, Table 2). A similar calculation for 1980–1 suggested a ratio of nearly three to one (*Hansard*, 28 March 1980, cols 725–6). For methods of calculating road track costs, see Ministry of Transport (1968).

15 The doubt comes from the Royal Commission's own figures. As an illustrative exercise, they calculate the annual cost of running a particular car in 1978 as £1,200. Later they show that the 'taxable charge' that the Inland Revenue would require an individual with a company car of this type and earning over £7,500 p.a. to add to his income before the latter is assessed for tax to be £1,150, a figure that is almost identical to the annual running costs of the car. If it is assumed that, if it had not provided the car, the firm would have paid the employee an amount equal to the car's annual running costs, then it appears as though the Inland Revenue's assessment of the value of this perk is about right; or, in other words, that, at least for employees earning over £7,500, there is no significant tax expenditure. It is not clear how this can be reconciled with the Royal Commission's statement quoted in the text.

PART THREE

The Strategy

CHAPTER 7

Equality and the Social Services

The implications of the findings ... therefore count as rather grave ones for the general strategy of egalitarian reform that has been widely adhered to among liberals and social democrats in modern Britain: briefly, the strategy of seeking to attack social inequalities via legislative and administrative measures of a piecemeal kind that can be carried through without venturing too far beyond the limits of 'consensus' politics. What our results would suggest – and the same point could indeed be made by reference to research on various other topics – is that this strategy grossly misjudges the resistance that the class structure can offer to attempts to change it: or, to speak less figuratively, the flexibility and effectiveness with which the more powerful and advantaged groupings in society can use the resources at their disposal to preserve their privileged positions. There is, in other words, a serious underestimation of the forces maintaining the situation in which change is sought, relative to the force of the measures through which, it is supposed, change can be implemented. *J. H. Goldthorpe*

Chapter 2 listed five different kinds of equality, each of which has appeared in one guise or another as an objective for public expenditure on the social services. The first of these was *equality of public expenditure*: public expenditure on the service concerned should be allocated equally per relevant individual. Then there was *equality of final income*: public expenditure should favour the poor, so as to bring their 'final incomes' (money income plus the value of the social services used) closer to those of the rich. The next was *equality of use*: relevant individuals should use the service equally. The fourth was *equality of cost*: all individuals should face the same personal costs of using the service, either in financial terms or in terms of the actual sacrifices involved. Finally, there was *equality of outcome*: as far as possible, all relevant individuals should have the same 'outcome' of the service concerned.

Have any of these objectives been achieved? Has public spending on any of the social services promoted equality in any of its interpretations? If not, can its direction or magnitude be changed in any way so as to improve matters? This chapter marshalls the evidence from Part Two to answer these questions.

Equality of Public Expenditure

To begin with, consider *health care*. Evidence concerning the distribution of National Health Service expenditure in Britain by occupational group suggests that such expenditure is distributed roughly equally per person. But, if differences in the groups' needs for the service are taken into account, a rather different picture emerges. The top socio-economic group (professionals, employers and managers) receive up to 40 per cent more NHS expenditure *per ill person* than the bottom group (semi- and unskilled manual workers), an inequality which remains even when the results are standardised for age and sex differences between the groups. Moreover, for a variety of reasons, it is likely that these estimates underestimate the actual inequality. In particular, the calculation assumed that the cost to the NHS of each GP consultation, hospital out-patient consultation and hospital in-patient day was the same for each socio-economic group, whereas there is evidence to suggest that in fact such costs are greater for consultations, etc., by the higher groups.

There are no reliable data on the distribution of public expenditure on health care by income group in Britain but there are some for the (very different) public health systems of other countries. Studies in Malaysia and Colombia show a broadly equal distribution of public expenditure per person (ill and not ill) between income groups, results which suggest that, since the poor are likely to experience much greater illness in those countries, then, as in Britain, the distributions per ill person would be markedly pro-rich. A study of the US Medicare programme (for the elderly) revealed that the higher the income group, the more was received per person eligible; the similar Medicaid programme (for the poor), while being confined only to the lower income groups, tended to benefit the better off within those groups.

Next, consider *education*. In Britain, the top fifth of the income distribution receives nearly three times as much public expenditure in education per household as the poorest fifth. If people are classified by occupation rather than income, a similar pattern appears, although not as pronounced. The top socio-economic group receives nearly 50 per cent more public expenditure per person in the relevant age range than the bottom group. This arises because, although they receive slightly less on primary and secondary education for pupils under 16, they receive substantially more on educating children over that age: twice as much for secondary pupils over 16, three times as much on further education, and over five times as much on university education. These results were not seriously affected if they were standardised for age and sex; but inclusion of the means-tested system of student awards did reduce slightly the inequality in the distribution of further and university education. Two other items of public expenditure in the education sector, the general subsidy to school meals and tax expenditures on private education, also favour those higher up the social scale; the means-tested element of school meals, not surprisingly, has a pro-poor distribution. Evidence from other countries mostly concerns public expenditure on further and university education; as in Britain, the relevant distribution is invariably pro-rich.

Thirdly, *housing*. There is no direct evidence on distribution in this area by occupational group in Britain, but there have been several studies of the distributional consequences of different policies by income group. Direct expenditures on council housing favour the poor since they have a higher proportion of council tenants and because, due to the rent rebate system, poorer tenants receive a larger subsidy than richer ones. But, with the exception of rent allowances to private tenants, other areas of housing expenditure are basically pro-rich. Of these the most significant are tax expenditures, that is, the variety of different tax reliefs for owner-occupiers. Since owner-occupation is far more prevalent in the higher income groups, and since these tax expenditures increase with the tax rate faced by a household and with the size of its mortgage (both of which are generally higher for the wealthy) the distribution is markedly pro-rich, to such an extent that it more than offsets the pro-poor distribution of council housing. As a result the net effect is that, overall, public expenditure on housing favours the better off, with the highest group receiving nearly twice as much as the lowest. Evidence concerning both public housing and tax expenditures in the United States and tax expenditures in Australia show a basically similar pattern to those for Great Britain.

Finally, *transport*. Again, most of the evidence is confined to Britain and to the distribution of public expenditure by income group. The richest fifth of the income distribution receive about ten times as much subsidy per household on rail travel and seventeen times as much on private transport as the poorest fifth. Even subsidies to bus operators tend to benefit the better off, although not nearly to the same extent. Adjustments for differences in household size do little to change the pattern for rail travel, but do reduce the share of the wealthy of expenditure on bus travel. Such evidence as is available concerning the distribution of private expenditure on buses by occupational group suggests that it is manual workers who are the principal beneficiaries.

Most public expenditure on the social services in Britain (and elsewhere) is thus distributed in a manner that broadly favours the higher social groups, whether 'higher' is defined in terms of income or occupation. The only established exceptions in developed countries are public housing, rent rebates and allowances, the US Medicaid system and means-tested elements in the education sector, all programmes that are confined by policy decision to people on low incomes.

Two points may be noted. First there are other researchers who have reached similar conclusions. Peter Townsend, in particular, in his recent massive survey of all aspects of poverty in the UK, including the distribution of the social services, concluded that 'contrary to common belief, fewer individuals in households with low than with high incomes received social services in kind of substantial value' (1979, p. 222). Second, the evidence reviewed is not only a problem for those committed to the aim of promoting equality in public expenditure, but also for those who subscribe to either the Marxist or the 'altruistic preferences of tax-payers' theories of the determinants of the welfare state. For, as noted in

Chapter 2, both of these require that the direct beneficiaries of public expenditure on the social services should be those lower down the social scale, a requirement that, as is apparent, is far from being met.

In fact, the evidence tends to support an alternative theory of the welfare state. It is possible that the overall gains that the higher groups have made due to public subsidisation of some at least of the social services outweigh any accompanying increases in their burden of taxation. If so, it is not too far-fetched to suggest that these elements of the welfare state owe their continued existence and support to the direct self-interest of the wealthy in the services they provide. In other words, public expenditure on the social services may be basically a device through which the better off use the general body of taxpayers to fund the consumption of a service that they would have purchased in any case, but which they otherwise would have had to pay for directly. But this is a speculation that will have to be left to researchers in the relevant area. For the purposes of this book, it is sufficient simply to repeat the basic conclusion of this section: public expenditure, in almost all the forms reviewed, is distributed in favour of the higher social groups.

Other Conceptions of Equality

It is apparent that, since public expenditure on each of the social services has a basically pro-rich distribution, it does not by itself promote *equality in final income.* The same evidence suggests that *equality of use* of each service has not been attained either. Indeed, the inequality in public expenditure in the case of education and health care understates the overall inequality in use, since the latter includes inequalities in the use of the private systems of education and health care.

Nor, in most cases, is there *equality of cost* as a result of public spending. The poor face greater costs of the Health Service than the rich because they often have further to travel to obtain the same quality of medical care, they have to rely on public transport and they have fewer telephones (for making consultations or appointments). Also, if they have to take time off work, they are more likely to lose income as a result, money which the very fact of their poverty means they can ill afford to lose. Similarly they face higher costs of using the education system than the rich. In particular, the sacrifices involved through the loss of income to a household if one of its members continues on at school instead of going out to work is likely to be substantially greater for poor households than rich ones.

In the case of housing, the situation is yet more perverse. Due in part to the vagaries of the tax system and in part to rising house values, owner-occupiers face lower money costs for equivalent housing than do council tenants or families renting from private landlords. Moreover, better-off owner-occupiers face lower costs than poorer ones. In some cases, wealthy owner-occupiers actually have *negative* costs, that is, they are not only paying nothing for their housing but are making a net financial gain from it.

Finally, in none of the areas concerned is there *equality of outcome*. In Part Two, the outcomes of the various services were taken to be health in the case of health care; qualifications, occupational mobility and earnings in the case of education; actual housing conditions in the case of housing; and travel in the case of transport. First, let us examine health. Unskilled manual workers' households report about twice as much illness as those of professionals. Their children are four times more likely to die in the first year of life, and about twice as likely to die in subsequent years. Overall, they can expect to live about five years less on average. Nor is the situation much better with respect to educational outcomes. The proportion of working-class sons who obtain at least one O-level is a quarter that of their middle-class contemporaries; there are similar differences in their chances of obtaining A-levels or a university degree. The sons of the middle class are over four times more likely themselves to have middle-class occupations than the sons of the working class; moreover, these occupations will pay twice as much as working-class ones.

Inequalities also persist in housing conditions. Proportionately, over twice as many working-class as middle-class households have one or more persons per room; about half as many have central heating; and half as many live in a detached or semi-detached house. Finally, there are substantial differences in travel; the higher social groups make more journeys than the lower ones, and on average travel over twice as far.

Is there Greater Equality?

Equality in public expenditure, final income, use, cost and outcome has not been achieved. But, as noted in Chapter 2, in some cases this might be too stringent a test. Rather, the aim of public spending on the social services could be interpreted as not necessarily the achievement of full equality, but rather that of greater equality. Whether it has succeeded in this respect is a much more difficult question to answer, partly because of the problem of deciding on the focus of comparison (greater equality than what?) and partly because of data difficulties. It does appear that in many key areas there has not been greater equality over time, at least. In particular, the differences in social class mortality rates, in the percentages of the sons of working-class and middle-class families going to university, and in the relative chances of working- and middle-class sons themselves being middle class, have all actually *widened* over the past fifty years or so.

Moreover, it is possible that in some cases, though by no means in all, there would be greater equality if there were no public expenditure on the service concerned. Suppose public expenditure on a particular social service was eliminated, and the resultant savings in government funds were used to increase everyone's money income equally (by, say, a combination of tax cuts and social security payments). Assume that nothing else changes – rather an implausible assumption, but one that is inevitable in counterfactual reasoning of this kind. Then, if the service concerned was council housing or rent rebates and allowances, there would be greater inequality in public expenditure and in final incomes; if it was the National Health Service there would be little effect. But, if the service was higher education, owner-occupation, or rail travel, there would be greater equality in both public expenditure and final income. Indeed, in these cases, there would be greater equality in final income if the savings were used to increase the disposable incomes of the rich by *more* than those of the poor – at least up to a point. For instance, the poor would be better off and the rich less well off if public expenditure on universities was eliminated and the rich given a reduction in tax that was up to five times that of the poor. The same is true of the elimination of the subsidies to owner-occupiers and to rail travel, except that the reduction in tax for the rich could be up to six times that for the poor in the case of owner-occupation and up to ten times in the case of rail travel, and the poor would still be better off as a result of the end of the subsidy.

It is even possible that there would be greater equality in use in some of these areas. For instance, raising the costs of university education would have the effect of reducing the competition for places, competition that, as was argued in Chapter 4, favours the middle class. Of course, to assess fully the overall effects on inequality in use it would be necessary to know not only the relevant increases in costs and in money incomes, but also the responses of the demand for education by different social groups to those increases (the relative price and income elasticities of demand, in technical language). What can be said is that, for most of the social services, there is no *a priori* reason to suppose that inequalities in use would necessarily increase as a result of the end of public subsidisation.

Overall, it is difficult to avoid the implication that the strategy of promoting equality through public expenditure on the social services has failed. It has failed to achieve full equality of whatever kind for most of the services reviewed. In those areas where data are available it has failed to achieve greater equality over time; and, in some cases, it is likely that there would be greater equality if there was no public expenditure on the service concerned.

Although these conclusions may come as a surprise to many people, it should be pointed out that there have been lone voices, on both the right and left of the political spectrum, who have reached broadly similar conclusions. University of Chicago economist George Stigler (1970) has proposed what he termed Director's Law (after Aaron Director, to whom he attributed it): the principal beneficiaries of the public budget are middle income groups, at the expense of the very rich and the very poor. Fellow economists Milton and Rose Friedman use Director's Law as part of their argument for abolishing much of the welfare state in their recent work on behalf of the market (1980, pp. 107, 111, 183). Further to the left, as long ago as 1958, Brian Abel-Smith argued that 'the major beneficiaries of [the creation of the Welfare State] have been the middle classes, that the middling income groups get more from the state than the lower income groups, that taxation often hits the poor harder than the well-to-do, and in general that the middle classes receive good standards of welfare while working people receive a spartan minimum' (pp. 55–6). Ten years later, Richard Titmuss claimed that the public provision of medical care, wage-related social security and education was 'not, by itself alone, enough ... This much we have learnt in the past two decades from the facts about inequalities in the distribution of income and wealth, and in our failure to close many gaps in differential access to, and effective utilisation of particular branches of our social services' (1968, pp. 134–5). And ten years after that, David Piachaud argued: 'much of current social policy contributes to the inequality which the government – through social security and taxation – then tries to moderate' (1979, p. 671).

Implications for Policy

Many will no doubt conclude from the above that public expenditure on the social services should be reduced, or even eliminated. And indeed there is little doubt that there are some areas which are difficult to justify maintaining expenditures at their present level on egalitarian grounds at least. These include public expenditure on higher education, tax subsidies to owner-occupiers, the free provision of road space in central cities and the subsidising of commuter rail services. As has been shown in the relevant chapters, their elimination would undoubtedly promote substantially greater equality of public expenditure. What would happen to the other aspects of inequality is difficult to predict precisely, because it depends on what happens to the tax revenues thus released. But, as was argued above, unless such revenues were used in a highly regressive fashion, there can be no presumption that inequalities in other areas will increase.

However, there are services where some of the relevant inequalities might be increased by reducing public expenditure, or where the losses in terms of other social objectives would be greater than the gain from a possible reduction in inequality. A prime example is the National Health Service which could be said to promote some degree of equality (although not full equality), and whose existence, as was argued in Chapter 3, can be justified according to a range of non-egalitarian criteria. In such cases, the appropriate policy appears to be to search for methods to reduce the relevant inequalities while retaining the service concerned in something like its present form.

What might such methods be? An obvious possibility is the extension of means tests. Not surprisingly, public expenditure on those elements of the social services that are means-tested did not systematically favour the better off, but rather the reverse. Inclusion of means-tested student grants in the estimates for the distribution of public expenditure on higher education reduced the inequality slightly. The school meals scheme, while offering a general subsidy to all which benefited the better off, has a means-tested element which partially offset this distribution. One of the criteria for allocating council houses is level of income, and as a result public expenditure on council housing tends to favour the less well off. Within the council house sector itself, there is a general subsidy which favours the more affluent tenant, and a means-tested rent rebate scheme which favours the less well off.

It might be thought, therefore, that the logical conclusion is to extend means-testing further. Means-tested charges could be introduced throughout the National Health Service, instead of being confined to a small range of services as at present. If it were decided to retain some public subsidy to higher education, means-tested grants for those staying on at school after the age of 16 could be introduced; and perhaps some means-tested system could be introduced for the pricing of public transport. This, it could be argued, would decrease the costs to the poor of the service concerned, relative to those faced by the rich, increase their use relative to that of the rich, and thereby promote greater equality of public expenditure, final income cost, use and – to the extent that outcomes are affected by use – outcomes as well.

But such arguments are too simplistic. Means tests are often regarded by those eligible as stigmatising and socially humiliating; people often have difficulties in finding out about a service and in filling out the requisite forms. The introduction of a means test into a previously 'free' service may therefore raise the non-monetary costs of using it even for those who can still obtain the service without charge. Hence everyone's use of the service may diminish, and inequalities in use may not change significantly, and if they do not alter, it is certain that inequalities in outcome will not.

That the presence of a means test can discourage the use of a service by the poor is well documented. Townsend's poverty study (1979) investigated a number of means-tested services and found few with a take-up rate of much more than half. Work by Meacher (1972), Lister (1974) and the National Consumer Council (1976) tells a similar story. Admittedly, not all means tests have this effect; in particular, official estimates put the take-up rate of the grants for students scheme at 100 per cent (National Consumer Council, 1976, p. 28), and that for rent rebates at over 75 per cent (Department of the Environment, 1980, p. 147). But these may be exceptional. Very few students in further or higher education come from poor households. The rent rebate scheme is directed only at council tenants who, as the National Consumer Council argues (1976, p. 43) 'are a highly concentrated and easily identifiable target group', and hence can be easily informed of the existence of the scheme.

Also, means tests have a variety of other problems associated with them. They can be inconsistent with one another (see Le Grand, 1975), and they exacerbate the so-called 'poverty trap' – the phenomenon that increases in individuals' earnings may render them ineligible for some means-tested benefits, and hence may actually reduce their standard of living. More generally, they can act as instruments of social control. 'The rules framing eligibility ... reflect values approved by society ... People who live rough, disrespect marriage, do not send their children regularly to school, are particular about the kind of employment they will accept, are in arrears with their rent, dress unusually or otherwise behave unconventionally will tend to be deprived of the benefits of means-tested services, even though the process by which this happens is indirect' (Townsend, 1979, p. 880).

In general, therefore, while there is no doubt that the further extension of means-testing in the social services would reduce inequalities in public expenditure, it is far from clear that other inequalities would thereby be reduced. Moreover, it might have other undesirable consequences, in particular through its effect on the poverty trap and on social divisions.[1]

Another possible method of achieving greater equality is to remove the individual's right to make the decision whether, and how much, to use the service. In areas of public expenditure outside the social services where the allocation of resources is controlled entirely by suppliers, such as police patrols, there is evidence to suggest that the distribution of expenditure, use and outcomes is equal or pro-poor (see Appendix A). In the one area within the social services where use is governed by law — education up to the age of 16 — again the distribution of public expenditure is (slightly) pro-poor. Moreover, as was noted in Chapter 4, it has been estimated that if the school-leaving age was raised this might reduce inequality in at least one aspect of educational outcome (earnings).

However, a widespread use of compulsory measures outside the education area (such as compulsory medical treatment for certain disorders) has obvious drawbacks. It would necessarily involve an erosion of civil liberties and might be extremely expensive to enforce. It would be socially divisive, since it would presumably be the poor who would have been 'compelled'; the well off would be using the service anyway. Further, it would not necessarily reduce inequality. Suppliers of both medical care and non-compulsory education already play a large role in determining how much potential users should receive: doctors through their decisions concerning treatment once a patient has contacted them, and teachers in further and higher education via the admissions procedures they employ. In each case, they tend to favour the better off in the decisions they make, doctors perhaps because they empathise better with middle-class patients and higher education teachers because the children of the middle class are better able to meet the criteria applied (performance in examinations, at interviews, etc.). All in all, it does not seem as though this 'solution' to the problem of creating greater equality is adequate either.

Unfortunately, the prospects for reform within the social services that involve neither means-testing nor reducing the role of the individual users seem equally gloomy. If services are provided at a uniform price to all who wish to use them, then it is inevitable that, unless the service is one of those rare commodities whose demand falls as income rises (that is, if it is what economists term an 'inferior' good), the wealthy will purchase more of it. The same is true even if the service is provided 'free'. For there will always be some financial costs associated with using it even if there is no direct charge (such as the cost of travel to the facility providing the service, or the income lost through the time involved in using it), costs that are likely to weigh more heavily on the poor than on the rich. Further, if the wealthy purchase more of a subsidised service, they will receive a larger public subsidy; and if the service contributes to a particular outcome they will have 'more' of whatever form that outcome takes. Hence there will inevitably be inequality of public expenditure, final income, use, costs and outcomes. This can be illustrated by experience outside the social services as well as within them. There is evidence, summarised in Appendix A, that subsidies to food, the performing arts, and the electricity and gas industries all favour the better off.

This is not to imply that there is no scope whatever for improvement within the existing framework of the social services. An example of a change in policy that is likely to have an effect on some of the relevant inequalities, and which does not involve an extension of means-testing or compulsion, is the current attempt to relocate health service facilities away from the rich South-East to the rest of the country. Yet it is difficult to believe that the impact even of measures such as this will be more than marginal. There is so much evidence from so many different areas that, almost regardless of the method of provision, the better off will always be able to make more effective use of even a freely provided service than the less well off. In that sense, the strategy of attempting to create equality through the provision of services that are free, or at a subsidised price to all, seems fundamentally misconceived.

Conclusion

Public expenditure on the social services has not achieved equality in any of its interpretations. Public expenditure on health care, education, housing and transport systematically favours the better off, and thereby contributes to inequality in final income. It has not created equality of cost (or equality of 'access'), and indeed in some cases has made cost differences worse; there persist substantial inequalities in outcomes. For several of the services there has not been even a reduction in the relevant inequalities over time. Nor does there seem to be much prospect of retrieving the situation through any piecemeal reform. Basically, the forces which created the inequalities in the first place and which perpetuate them seem to be too strong to be resisted through indirect methods such as public expenditure on the social services. Rather, the strategy of equality has to be aimed at tackling those forces directly, an argument that is developed in the final chapter.

Note to Chapter 7

1 For a stimulating discussion of most of the relevant issues in the context of one particular means-tested programme, see Davies (1978). Interestingly, he concludes that, for a variety of reasons, means-testing in the programme concerned (free school meals) is 'less objectionable than many other means-tested benefits' (p. 206).

CHAPTER 8

The Alternative

If we want to redistribute income, the most effective strategy is probably still to redistribute income. *C. Jencks*

I am sure that the power of vested interests is vastly exaggerated compared with the gradual encroachment of ideas. Not, indeed, immediately, but after a certain interval; for in the field of economic and political philosophy there are not many who are influenced by new theories after they are twenty-five or thirty years of age, so that the ideas which civil servants and politicians, and even agitators apply to current events are not likely to be the newest. But, sooner or later, it is ideas, not vested interests, which are dangerous for good or evil. *J. M. Keynes*

The failure of public expenditure on the social services to achieve equality can be explained primarily by its inability successfully to counteract the influence of the more fundamental social and economic inequalities that still pervade British society. In particular, as will be established in the first section of this chapter, if the pattern of inequality associated with public provision is viewed as a whole, one salient feature emerges; that is, the importance of inequalities in private money income. Hence, for any strategy of equality to succeed, it has to tackle these inequalities directly. To do so, it has to confront the ideology which lies behind them, an ideology whose basis is discussed in the second section of the chapter.

The Role of Money Income

The review of the evidence in Part Two suggested that inequalities in public expenditure, use, costs and outcomes in the social services arise in large part because of inequalities in money incomes. Consider, first, inequalities in cost. In some cases, the poor actually face higher financial costs than the rich. Due to their low incomes they find it more difficult to purchase houses and hence benefit from the reductions in costs that accrue to owner-occupiers. They live in areas poorly endowed with social service facilities, and hence have to travel further, and by more inconvenient means, if they wish to use the service concerned. Even where the financial costs are the same or less (as with means-tested services) the sacrifices for the poor may be as great as, or more than, those for the rich. Large expenditures by rich individuals may cost them less in terms of unmet wants or needs than smaller expenditures by poor individuals.

If it is assumed, as seems reasonable, that people take account of the costs involved when deciding whether or not to use a service, then inequalities in such costs, other things being equal, will create inequalities in use and thereby generally in public expenditure. These too are therefore income-related. Even if the inequalities in use arise primarily from differences in the benefits that people perceive from using a service rather than in its costs, income may still play an important role. In the case of health care and education, it was observed how income could affect tastes and attitudes and thus affect the perception of benefits from both of these items of public consumption.

From the evidence presented in the relevant chapters, it appears that inequalities in outcomes may also be heavily influenced by differences in money incomes. This is partly because there are income-related inequalities in the use of the services that affect outcomes. More importantly, in some cases it is also because other factors affecting outcomes are heavily influenced by income. For instance, nutrition seems to be a more important determinant of health than medical care, and nutrition is closely associated with income. A child's socio-economic background appears to be a more important determinant of his or her educational achievement than education itself, and the level of a household's income is a key element in its socio-economic status.

It appears therefore as though a more promising way than those discussed in the last chapter of achieving equality *of whatever kind* would be through equalising incomes. Greater equality of incomes would lead to greater equality of costs (in terms of the sacrifices involved and sometimes in money terms as well). This in turn would lead to greater equality of use and hence of public expenditure. It would also contribute importantly to greater equality of outcomes. A more equal society in terms of income would be one where more equal treatment was offered for equal need, where inequalities in health, in education and in educational outcomes were reduced and where the gaps in housing and travel opportunities were diminished. The strategy of equality therefore should be one of achieving greater equality of money income.

Contrary to popular belief, inequalities in income are still considerable. In 1976, the top 20 per cent of the population received 42 per cent of the total national income while the bottom 20 per cent received 6 per cent. Even if income tax is taken into account, the gap narrows only slightly; in 1976 the top 20 per cent received nearly 40 per cent of after-tax income and the bottom 20 per cent under 8 per cent. Inequalities in wealth are yet more pronounced, with the top 1 per cent owning a quarter of total marketable wealth, and the top 20 per cent over three-quarters. Moreover, there is evidence that there has been little reduction in some of these inequalities over the past thirty years. For instance, the share of the national income received by the bottom half of the population has not changed since 1949.[1]

The ways in which differences in income and wealth could be reduced are legion. They range from modest reforms to the social security system, through proposals for a negative income tax or social dividend, to, at the extreme, the forcible expropriation of property. There is not the space here to examine properly the relative merits of all the different methods; an elementary attempt to do so for some of them can be found in Le Grand and Robinson (1976, Ch. 9).

Instead, it seems more appropriate to concentrate upon a more fundamental issue, the ideological barriers to greater economic equality, since these barriers were in part responsible for the instigation of the strategy of equality with which this book has been concerned. Many of its proponents believed that public expenditure on the social services was perhaps the only way to achieve a significant measure of redistribution. Indeed, the basic philosophical rationale for many of the egalitarian objectives put forward to guide policy towards the social services is difficult to understand, except in this light. In particular, the objectives of equality of public expenditure, of use and of outcome only really make sense as limited (and thereby supposedly more acceptable) versions of the underlying aim of greater overall equality. Public expenditure on the social services was thus in part designed to avoid the nettle of income redistribution; in other words, an attempt to achieve such redistribution via the back door. As we have seen, however, it was inadequate for the task. Indeed, through convincing people (wrongly) that a substantial measure of redistribution was taking place, it may even have confused the basic aim.

None the less, it has to be acknowledged that there is a greater measure of agreement on achieving some kind of equality within the social services than there is on the wider issue of money income redistribution. Hence any strategy of equality that has as its main objective such redistribution has to make some attempt to command a wider consensus. To do so, it has to challenge the ideology of inequality – the set of beliefs and values that underpins economic inequality and which is the major obstacle to any attempt to reduce it.

The Ideology of Inequality

The ideology of inequality comprises two, rather different, sets of beliefs. One is that the present structure of inequalities is basically fair, that people deserve the income they receive, and that, by and large, the rich are deserving and the poor undeserving. The other does not necessarily hold the present structure to be fair, but will none the less oppose moves towards greater economic equality on the grounds that (1) there is already a substantial degree of equality (perhaps even too much) and (2) to attempt to reduce inequality yet further would have disastrous consequences for any other objectives which society may have, such as diversity, economic growth or liberty.

Now it might be thought that the divide between those who subscribe to either, or both, of these sets of beliefs and committed egalitarians is basically one of value, and hence cannot be bridged by rational discussion. There is some element of truth in this. For instance, there are substantial differences in the relative values that each side would attach to the claims of individual liberty and of social justice. But many of the differences between the two ideologies are actually matters of fact (or of factual interpretation) and thus are more amenable to debate. The statements that there is already a substantial measure of equality, or that there exists a trade-off between equality of economic reward, on the one hand, and efficiency, diversity and liberty, on the other, are assertions which are, in principle at least, open to empirical verification. An examination of the facts can even throw some light upon the apparently hopelessly value-laden question as to the basic fairness or otherwise of the existing income distribution, so long as there is a basic consensus on the meaning of fairness. Unfortunately, there is not the space here to discuss major philosophical issues such as these in detail. What follows therefore is simply a brief outline of the principal ideas, beginning with the question of fairness.

Equality and Fairness

The first, and perhaps most important, issue to tackle is whether the current distribution of economic resources is fair or just. A basic belief that it is indeed fair is an essential element of the ideology of inequality. It is widely held, implicitly or explicitly, that people have 'earned' their incomes, and that the state has no right to take their money or even to give them more. It is manifest, for example, in the common attitude that accepts as normal, or even praiseworthy, the avoidance or evasion of taxation – considered as protecting one's 'own' money – while condemning in the severest terms social security fraud – viewed as trying to obtain 'other people's'. It is part of the reason why the poor often refuse welfare benefits to which they are entitled, for they feel that they have not 'earned' them, a feeling that in turn led to many of the services designed to help the poor being set up in the form of being free to all, with the consequences for equality that have been seen in earlier chapters.

To tackle properly the ideology of inequality, therefore, it is necessary to question the belief that the present distribution of income is fair. To do so, it is necessary to see if there is a consensus on what is meant by fair. Elsewhere I have argued at some length that there is a consensus definition of fairness;[2] what follows is an informal summary of the basic idea.

Suppose we observe three individuals, A, B and C. B and C have the same income, but A has a higher income than both. We are informed that the reason why B's income is depressed relative to A's is because there are imperfections in the market which prevent him or her from receiving the same wage as A. (An example could be if he or she were black and employers had a taste for discrimination.) C, on the other hand, faces the same wage rate as A, but has a lower income because he or she has decided to take more time off from work than A. They have the same job opportunities, they are equally aware of the advantages of working, including receiving a higher income, but C prefers to trade those advantages in return for a greater amount of leisure.

Now both B and C are equally deprived relative to A in income terms. But the degree of unfairness inherent in their deprivation seems to be different. C has voluntarily 'deprived' himself or herself of income, in return for increased leisure; hence it is difficult to regard the disparity between his or her income and A's as, *ipso facto*, unfair. B, on the other hand, has not chosen to be relatively deprived but has been prevented by factors beyond his or her control from raising his or her income. Here inequity does seem to be present. Although the differences between the incomes of the two individuals and that of A are the same, our judgements concerning the respective fairness of their situations are different, a difference which arises from our perception of the degrees of choice involved.

Now suppose we realised that some of the evidence about the situation with which we had been supplied was incorrect. Specifically, imagine we learned that the reason why B received a lower wage rate than A was not because of imperfections in the market, but because he or she is less highly skilled than A. Moreover, we were informed, both B and A had exactly the same opportunity to acquire those skills by undergoing training, and both were equally aware of the cost and benefits that would result if they trained. In that case our judgement as to the inequity of the situation might change. We may now feel that B chose to have a lower income than A, not because he or she has a higher rate of 'trading-off' income for leisure at the going wage rate (as does C) at least in the current period, but because he or she exercised his or her preferences at an earlier period. As a result, we may now feel that the difference between A's and B's income (as between A's and C's) is not inequitable.

Suppose we then received a further bit of information. We discovered that the reason why C has a higher rate of trade-off between leisure and income than A is because he or she has an invalid child and hence has to spend time at home in order to look after this child. We might then say, well, the disparity in incomes between A and C does now appear unfair: A has a higher income than C, but this is not really the result of choice on C's part.

Note what has happened. Our judgement about the fairness of the situation has undergone a number of changes and indeed has ended in a complete reversal of our initial judgement. This has occurred, not because the disparities in income have changed, nor because our basic values have changed, but because at each stage we acquired new information concerning the freedom of choice each individual had in determining his situation.

The element that is crucial to determining the fairness or otherwise of a situation thus seems to be the existence or otherwise of choice. For, as is apparent from the example considered, *our judgement as to the degree of unfairness inherent in a given income distribution is dependent on the degree to which we see that distribution as an outcome of individual choices.*

There are many other examples which can reinforce the point. This conception of fairness is implicit in the judgement that inequalities of cost are inequitable. But it is also implicit in the views of many of those who advocate equality of outcome, for the reason they do so is because they believe differences in allocations usually arise not through individual choices but because of factors beyond individual control. It is often regarded as unfair if one child receives less education than another because his parents had a lower socio-economic status, again an example of restricted choice. Under most social security systems those who resign from their job voluntarily are not eligible for unemployment pay. The judgement seems to be that it is not fair to pay social security to those who have voluntarily decided to reduce their income, a judgement that follows directly if fairness is related to choice.

If this argument is accepted, then the question as to whether incomes in our society are fair becomes essentially an empirical one. For it will depend on the extent to which the income distribution arises from factors within individual control; not always an easy question to answer in practice but one that has considerably more potential for eventual resolution than a clash of values.

In a market economy, individuals' incomes depend on the resources (labour, land or capital) which they 'own', the amount of those resources they supply to the productive process, and on the price they receive per unit of resource supplied. Now, the price of a resource is determined by the supply and demand for that resource and perhaps – particularly in the case of the wage rate – by traditional custom. All of these factors are, by and large, beyond the control of any one individual. The resources owned by individuals derive from two sources: they were either inherited or accumulated. When individuals receive wealth (land or capital) through inheritance they inherit labour resources, via the genetic structure with which they are endowed. On this inherited base, they can accumulate more: in the case of wealth, through investing their inherited wealth or by saving out of their income; in the case of labour, by accumulating 'human' capital (educational skills, job training and so on). Now it seems reasonable to suppose that the portion of an individual's resources which is inherited is predominantly beyond individual control. Certainly, no one can affect his or her genetic endowment; and, although there are reported cases of people influencing their inheritance of wealth (children defying their parents, young couples persuading old ladies whom they have been looking after to change wills in their favour), this does not conform to the general run of experience. The process of accumulation, however, can be viewed as more under individual control. People do appear to make choices about their savings behaviour and about their education. Yet even here the choice is often constrained. The rate of return to be earned on large investments is higher than on small ones because risk can be spread; hence those who begin with a sizeable sum are better placed to accumulate more. As we saw in Chapter 4, many people have little choice about continuing their education; outside pressures predominate. Even the desire to accumulate (to save, to acquire an education) will depend at least in part on parental upbringing, and other environmental conditioning, again factors beyond individual control.

Moreover, at least in so far as wealth is concerned, there is evidence to suggest that inheritance plays a more important role in determining large fortunes than accumulation. In recent years, Professor Harbury and his associates have put in much painstaking work in tracing the fathers of those who have died leaving large fortunes. They found that 60 per cent of top male wealth-leavers were preceded by fathers who were at least moderately rich (Harbury and Hitchens, 1979). The self-made millionaire is an important element of the ideology of inequality but he is as mythological as many of its other 'facts'.

The other determinant of income is the proportion of an individual's resources that he or she supplies to the productive process. At first sight this may appear to be primarily a matter of choice, a view often expressed when the unemployed are described as work-shy or lazy. Yet here again people's choices are often heavily constrained. For some there is no work available. Others can work if they wish but only at menial, uncomfortable jobs. Many have commitments at home, which severely curtail their work opportunities; a problem that is particularly acute for single parents. Individuals are also often restricted in their work by their states of health. All of these factors will limit individual incomes; all are, in large part, beyond individual control.

So the incomes people receive are heavily influenced, if not completely dominated, by factors beyond individual control. In that case it is difficult to argue that the current distribution of income is fair − at least in the sense that the term is generally used. The ideology of inequality has lost one of its major supports.

But this is by no means the only element of that ideology. Many of its supporters would acknowledge that distribution of income that is largely determined by the market is unfair (see, for instance, Joseph and Sumption, 1979, p. 95), but would none the less maintain that it is quite undesirable to attempt to alter it. For to do so would damage society's ability to achieve its other objectives. Let us examine these arguments in more detail.

Equality and Other Objectives

It is often claimed that the pursuit of equality damages society in a number of significant ways. Among other things, it is supposed to stifle diversity and promote cultural drabness, to interfere seriously with the growth of the economy; and place massive restrictions on individual liberty. The argument is often sustained by bleak descriptions of a totalitarian society in which, in the name of equality, all individual differences and liberties are suppressed and which is stagnant economically and culturally.

The argument that greater equality of economic reward would promote sameness and discourage variety is, as de Lone (1979, p. 179) points out, based on a confusion between inequality and diversity. Equality before the law or equality of voting rights as between one individual and another does not imply that they have the same tastes, the same sense of humour, the same political preferences, the same aesthetic judgements, the same psychological make-up, or the same physiology. Why then should equality of economic reward? Indeed, such equality might promote the flowering of individual differences of character, for as Tawney (1964) argues 'differences of personal quality ... in England ... tend to be obscured or obliterated behind differences of property or income' (p. 48).

The supposed trade-off between equality and economic growth is one of the major weapons in the non-egalitarian's armoury. High income tax rates are supposed to discourage work effort, as are welfare payments to the poor; wealth taxation allegedly discourages saving, and hence the formation of capital. But it is difficult to sustain any of these propositions on *a priori* grounds. There is no theoretical reason for supposing that high income tax rates necessarily discourage work effort. It is true that a high marginal tax rate lowers the opportunity cost or 'price' of leisure, and, as with any commodity whose price is reduced, thereby encourages people to consume more of it (and thus do less work). But, on the other hand, it also lowers peoples' incomes, and thereby may induce them to work harder so as to maintain their standard of living. These two effects – the substitution and income effects, in economists' parlance – operate in opposite directions, and their net effect is impossible to predict from theory alone. Similarly, wealth taxation may discourage people from saving, as it raises the price of saving. On the other hand, it may encourage people to save more in order to maintain their wealth against the encroachments of the tax. For most welfare schemes, the income and substitution effects operate in the same direction. Hence it is possible to predict that in these cases their net effect will be to discourage work, but the theory gives us no indication by how much.

The empirical evidence on the incentives question is usefully reviewed in Atkinson and Stiglitz (1980, pp. 48–59, 91–5). Surveys of attitude towards taxation in both the United States and the UK suggest that it plays little part in determining people's work and spending decisions; but survey information of this kind is of questionable reliability. Evidence from observed behaviour is in principle more acceptable than surveys, but in practice such studies as have been done on both the incentive to work and to save encounter severe methodological difficulties, and, moreover, produce conflicting results. What can be said is that, despite many attempts, no one has successfully proved that increasing taxation will definitely reduce either work effort or savings, and hence that there is no necessary trade-off between greater equality and greater work effort.

The (presumed disastrous) effect of the pursuit of equality on liberty is a favourite theme of libertarian thinkers, such as F. A. Hayek and Milton Friedman. Yet it is difficult to see the exact route which this supposed phenomenon is supposed to take. A society where economic rewards are more equal than they are in contemporary Britain is not necessarily a totalitarian society, with all property expropriated, all individuals regimented, and all labour centrally directed. Certainly, the instruments most likely to be used to promote greater equality, such as taxation of high incomes or of inheritance, do involve some curtailment of liberty, in the sense that people cannot avoid the tax except by changing their behaviour in some way. But a society with tax rates on, say, income and inheritance substantially higher than those currently prevailing in the UK is still a long way from Orwell's Airstrip One.

None of this is to deny the possibility that *at some point* in the pursuit of equality, some of the dire consequences predicted by libertarian thinkers might become manifest. For instance, if full economic equality were imposed such that all individuals received the same income whether or not they worked, there would doubtless be a (substantial) drop in national output. But most egalitarians would stop well short of advocating full equality of this kind. This is not because they are inconsistent; rather, it is because they do not believe that greater equality should be pursued at all points and at all times, regardless of the costs in terms of other objectives (in technical language, they do not have a lexicographic ordering of objectives). It is quite consistent to acknowledge the undesirability of full equality while at the same time believing that a degree of economic inequality well below that which currently obtains is desirable, because to get there would involve relatively little cost in terms of other objectives.

The experience of other countries suggests that greater equality in income, wealth or earnings does not necessarily harm either economic growth or liberty. The post-tax-and-transfer distribution of both income and wealth is significantly more equal in Sweden than in the UK. The United States has roughly the same distribution of income, but a far more equal distribution of wealth. Germany and the Netherlands have similar distributions of income and wealth, but greater equality in (industrial) earnings.[3] Yet none of these countries is noticeably inferior to Britain in terms of political freedom, and all are considerably superior in economic performance.

Conclusion

A major reason why the strategy of equality discussed in earlier chapters took the form that it did was because of a reluctance by some of its proponents to confront the ideology of inequality. As a result, a system was established that aimed to promote equality within a limited sphere. But, by leaving basic economic inequality relatively untouched, it sowed the seeds of its own failure.

The lesson is clear. If greater equality of whatever kind is desired, it is necessary to reduce economic inequality. To do this successfully, however, it is necessary to reduce the hold of the ideology of inequality on people's values and beliefs, and this can only be done by challenging the factual underpinnings of that ideology. These underpinnings are weak. Differences in people's incomes arise in large part because of factors beyond their control; hence these differences are rarely fair. To reduce them would therefore serve the cause of social justice; moreover, there is little evidence that this would damage other causes, such as those of diversity, economic growth or liberty. Most of the arguments against reducing economic inequality are based on dubious premises, and it is important that no strategy of equality should, even implicitly, accept them.

I do not wish to imply by the foregoing that a successful assault on the ideology of inequality will remove all obstacles to the redistribution of income. For there is, of course, another major barrier – the self-interest of the wealthy. They will wish to protect their standard of living, their privileges and their power. Moreover, the very fact of their wealth confers on them the ability to defend their position. They can buy media outlets which offer a view of the world that reinforces the ideology of inequality; they can threaten or actually undertake activities which undermine any attempt to deprive them of their wealth (by, say, firing troublesome workers, or emigrating to tax havens); and *in extremis* they can buy armies or police forces to defend them.

But the barriers to equality do not rest on self-interest alone.

Ideology is a much more important determinant of social processes than is often supposed. To understand what people believe is crucial to understand the way they behave; and to change the way they behave, it is crucial to change what they believe. Indeed ideology can often override self-interest. People can be induced by ideology to perform all manner of bizarre activities that in no way further their own interests. Indeed, at the extreme, they can be persuaded to kill themselves in battle. More to the point, a change in beliefs can even induce people to reduce their power and privilege. The extension of the franchise to the non-propertied classes and to women over the past century and a half, for instance, can be explained not just as an attempt to 'buy off' revolution but as an acceptance that the ideological underpinnings of the opposition had collapsed. Keynes put the argument well when he said in the quote at the beginning of this chapter, 'the power of vested interests is vastly exaggerated compared with the gradual encroachment of ideas' (Keynes, 1936, p. 383).

The strategy of equality through public provision has failed. It failed primarily because it implicitly accepted the ideology of inequality. Any alternative strategy has to have as an essential part an attack on that ideology; otherwise it too will fail. But if it does make the attempt and if the attempt succeeds, then there is a chance that the divisions that have plagued British society for centuries, and that have led to the inequalities documented in this book, will at last be eliminated.

Notes to Chapter 8

1 All figures in this paragraph are from the Royal Commission on the Distribution of Income and Wealth (1980).
2 See Le Grand (1981). This also includes discussions of other recent contributions to the area, including the major works of John Rawls and F. Hayek.
3 *Sources:* Stark (1977, p. 156), Harrison (1979, p. 34, Table 6, p. 50, Table 12) and Saunders and Marsden (1979, p. 8).

Appendices

Studies of the Distribution of Public Expenditure

The first section of this appendix lists some published studies of the distribution of public expenditure that are not discussed in the main text. It reviews some of the evidence produced and draws attention to the implications of that evidence for the general conclusions of this book. The second section discusses the major methodological criticisms that have been made of the procedures followed by studies of the distribution of public expenditure, and again considers their implications for the book's conclusions. In parts of this section the analysis is at a level that will not be accessible to those without some background in economics.

The Studies

Most of the empirical investigations of the distribution of public expenditure are of one of two kinds. There are 'macro-studies', which investigate the impact of the government budget as a whole, estimating the distribution of as many forms of public expenditure as those undertaking the work considered practical, together with the distribution of taxation. And there are 'micro-studies', which investigate principally the distribution of one particular form of public expenditure.

The macro-studies begin with, for Britain, a pioneering investigation of the distribution of taxation and public expenditure in 1937 by Barna (1945); similar studies for later years include Weaver (1950), Peacock and Browning (1954), Cartter (1955), Nicholson (1964), Merrett and Monk (1966), Nicholson and Britton (1976) and the estimates based on Nicholson's 1964 work that have been produced for each year since 1957 by the Central Statistical Office (CSO), of which the most recent is CSO (1981). Equivalent studies for other countries are mostly confined to the United States; recent examples are Gillespie (1965), Musgrave, Case and Leonard (1974), Reynolds and Smolensky (1977) and Ruggles (1979).

Except for the CSO studies, the relevant evidence from which has been considered in the main text, the results of the macro-studies have generally not been examined in this book. This is because they offer little of what might be termed 'primary' evidence, that is, evidence derived from surveys of the actual use of public services. Instead, for their allocations of public expenditure they rely either on primary data provided by the micro-studies or, where that is absent, upon simple assumptions concerning the distribution for particular services (such as equal expenditure per head). In passing it might be noted that, although the CSO estimates have been widely criticised, they are significantly better than the other macro-studies in this respect, being based on an actual survey of use (the Family Expenditure Survey). Indeed, they are the more remarkable for being produced annually in a comprehensive and easily digestible form by the British government's statistical service. No other government produces anything remotely comparable.

Micro-studies of distribution that have not been already discussed in the main text include investigations of the distribution of subsidies designed to hold down the prices of food and of the products of some nationalised industries, the distribution of subsidies to the performing arts, and the distribution of resources for the police and fire services. To begin with *price subsidies*. Witt and Newbould (1976) have investigated the distribution of those subsidies introduced by the Labour government immediately following their election victory in 1974. The subsidies were concentrated upon bread, butter, milk, cheese, flour and tea. Witt and Newbould used data from the Family Expenditure Survey on the expenditure by household on those items to calculate the value of these subsidies for a married couple with two children in each of several different income groups for the fiscal year 1974–5. They found that a 'rich' family (living on £100–£120 per week, slightly more than twice the average industrial wage) received between 38 and 45 per cent more subsidy than a 'poor' family (living on £30–£35 per week, two thirds of the average wage), the exact amount varying from month to month. Calculating the benefits to families in all income groups and aggregating them, they estimated that 'sixty three per cent of government expenditures on food subsidies went to families with incomes above the national average' (p. 32). The message is clear: food subsidies benefited the better off to a greater extent than the less well off.

Food subsidisation (along with that of other commodities) is widespread in socialist countries, and it is interesting to see that the same pattern appears there. György Szakolczai (1980) of the Research Institute of Applied Computer Sciences in Budapest has investigated the Hungarian system of redistribution through the use of commodity prices. He used a variety of means to calculate the 'real' costs of production of certain commodities and compared these with the prices faced by consumers. He found that for food and 'services' (including health care, education and transport), the average cost per unit exceeded the price of that unit, indicating subsidisation, while for most other commodities consumer prices exceeded the real cost. The extent of food and services subsidisation, however, was so great and the proportion of those commodities consumed by the better off so large that the net impact of the whole system was, once again, to discriminate against the poor.

Another area of price subsidy in Britain concerned the nationalised industries producing electricity, gas and coal. As part of its anti-inflation policy in the early 1970s, the government held down the prices of these commodities and paid compensation to the industries to meet their resultant deficits. The sums involved were large: in 1974–5, for instance, they amounted to over £1,000 million. If it is assumed that the benefits from such subsidies accrued in direct proportion to households' private expenditure on the products of these industries, then the distribution of the subsidies can be inferred from the distribution of the private expenditure. Calculations of such distributions (Le Grand, 1978) for coal, gas, electricity and postal services and telephones showed – not too surprisingly – that the rich spent more on average on each of them, with the exception of coal. Hence it seems that they benefited more from these price restraint policies than did the poor.

Two Australian economists (Throsby and Withers, 1979) calculated the distributional effects of *subsidies to the performing arts* in Australia and the UK. Although such subsidies are small as a proportion of public expenditure in the UK (expenditure on arts and libraries comprised about 0.5 per cent of total public expenditure in 1978–9), they form a large part of the income of most of the organisations involved. For instance, in 1971 40 per cent of the income of dramatic arts companies in the UK came from public funds. The equivalent figure for dance and opera companies was 53 per cent, and for orchestras a staggering 84 per cent (*ibid.*, p. 148, Table 9.3).

Throsby and Withers used survey data on households' private expenditure on entertainment for their estimates, therefore assuming that the distribution of public expenditure matched that of private expenditure (data were taken for the UK from the 1976 Family Expenditure Survey and for Australia from an unpublished Morgan Gallup poll). Unfortunately they were unable to obtain data on households' private expenditure for the subsidised arts alone. The closest categories were, for Australia, expenditure on 'live theatre' and for the UK the even broader one of expenditure on 'theatres, sporting events and other entertainments'. Hence their estimates are far from reliable.

None the less, for what they are worth, they show substantial disparities. In the UK, the top 20 per cent of households received over 40 per cent of public expenditure, while the bottom 25 per cent received just 4 per cent. In Australia, the top 12 per cent received over 30 per cent of the expenditure and the bottom 15 per cent received 3 per cent. Moreover, since the better off constitute a higher proportion of the audience for the subsidised performing arts than of the audience for other forms of entertainment (Baumol and Bowen, 1966, Table IV-2, p. 91), these estimates are likely to underestimate the inequality, particularly for the UK.

Police and fire services are often considered to be pure public goods and hence not allocable to specific groups. But they do differ from public goods such as national defence in one important particular, viz., they are often geographically specific. A policeman on his beat in one area of the city does not necessarily affect equally all residents in other areas, still less residents of other cities. Weicher (1971) uses this fact to argue that the services of police patrolmen at least cannot be described as a pure public good. Instead, he claims that geography can act as an exclusion device, and hence that these services can be allocated in different amounts to specific individuals. On this basis he investigated the distribution of police patrolmen in Chicago by district, found that more were allocated to low income districts, and argued that the distributional pattern therefore favoured the poor. Bloch (1974) investigated the distribution of police services between a rich and a poor district of Washington, D.C., and concluded that by a variety of different measures, equality was being achieved. Police 'inputs' were distributed equally, and their 'outputs', as measured either by property crime rates or by the clear-up rate (the proportion of crimes solved), were almost equal.

Lineberry (1975, 1977) reached a similar conclusion for fire protection. Investigating the distribution of these services for San Antonio, Texas, he observed that middle-class districts were poorly served relative to working-class districts, and concluded that 'the hypothesis [of the poor doing badly in the distribution of these services] does not fare well in examining empirically the distribution ... in one American city' (1975, p. 79).

The conclusions concerning police services could be challenged on the grounds that the fact that distribution of police patrols favours the poor (as in Weicher's case) or is equally distributed (as in Bloch's) does not necessarily imply that the use of (and hence public expenditure on) those services is similarly distributed. Many would argue that poor families make little or no use of police 'protection', that they regard policemen at best with indifference or at worst as actual enemies. Moreover, police patrols may be allocated to poor areas, not so much for the use of those areas but to reduce the possibility of their residents engaging in criminal activities against the residents of rich areas.

Particularly after the recent troubles in British cities, it is clear that the first of these points carries some weight, although its importance might be exaggerated. After all, as Weicher says, the poor are 'disproportionately the victims of crime' (p. 208), and there are likely to be many members of a poor community who would welcome a police presence. Weicher tested for the second possibility by examining the relationship between the number of patrolmen in an area and the difference between its mean income and that of neighbouring areas. If the possibility were correct, he suggested, areas with low incomes relative to their neighbours should have large numbers of patrolmen in order to inhibit their residents from becoming criminals; similarly, areas with high incomes relative to their neighbours should have relatively few. In fact, the only correlation he found was statistically insignificant and operated in the reverse direction, a result which, if it means anything, implies that patrolmen are actually allocated to districts to benefit the residents of those districts.

Of the areas investigated, therefore, the only ones that do not necessarily appear to have a pro-rich distribution are police patrols and fire services. They are also the only services among those reviewed whose allocation is determined primarily by policy decisions made by the suppliers of the service. It appears, therefore, that, as with the social services, the distribution of public expenditure on those commodities whose use is not confined to specific groups by policy – such as the general subsidies on food, electricity, gas and the performing arts – will tend to favour the better off.

Some Methodological Issues

Many of the problems specific to the studies on the social services have been discussed in the main text. However, there are a number of general methodological difficulties which apply to almost all studies of the distribution of public expenditures (both macro- and micro-). These have been extensively discussed by a number of authors including Peacock and Shannon (1968), Prest (1968), Aaron and McGuire (1970), Webb and Sieve (1972), Peacock (1974), Boreham and Semple (1976), Field, Meacher and Pond (1977) and O'Higgins (1980). The points raised by these writers may be grouped under the headings of *inclusion, incidence, valuation* and *comparison.*

Inclusion

Much of the criticism has concerned the services included or omitted in the macro-studies investigating the overall distributive impact of the government budget. This is not directly relevant to the studies examined here, and hence will not be considered further. However, there is one important area of omission which does apply to many of the studies discussed – that of capital expenditure.

The omission of the capital expenditure on a particular service in a given year from estimates of the distribution of public expenditure in that year is usually justified on the grounds that the benefits from that expenditure accruing to individuals using the services in the future should not be allocated to those using them in the present (see, for example, Peretz, 1975, p. 9). This argument has been criticised on two grounds. First, some parts of what is generally considered to be current expenditure in certain areas (such as education and health care) also yield benefits that accrue in the future; therefore consistency would require that these too should be omitted (Boreham and Semple, 1976, p. 292). Second, the argument implies that elements of past capital expenditure should be allocated as well as current expenditure, a procedure that is rarely followed (Boreham and Semple, 1976, p. 274; Peretz, 1975, p. 9).

The first criticism is slightly misplaced. If the intention is to calculate the distribution of the public expenditure undertaken in a particular year, it is incorrect to omit some of that expenditure (whether nominally 'current' or 'capital') on the grounds that it yields benefits in the future. Rather, the procedure should be to allocate such expenditure (subject to appropriate discounting) to those who are going to receive the future benefits. These may be the current users of the service (as in the case of education), or they may be future users (as in the case of a motorway in the process of construction). The second criticism is more legitimate. Strictly speaking, public expenditure on a particular service in a given year should (although it rarely does) include the opportunity cost of the capital used (its value in an alternative use); and therefore any estimate of the distribution of that expenditure should also include the distribution of that opportunity cost.

All the studies of the distribution of public expenditure in this book omit capital expenditure in the current year. However, this would only be a problem for the conclusions derived from these studies in the main text if, under existing policies, the distribution of such expenditure was significantly different from that of current expenditure. Since this would require the distribution of future users of the relevant services to be different from the distribution of present users this seems unlikely. As far as past capital expenditure is concerned, as discussed in Chapter 5, the opportunity cost of capital is taken into account in the housing studies of Rosenthal (1977), Hughes (1979) and Robinson (1980). It is not included in the studies for health care and education, but since if it were included it would be allocated to current users in the same way as current expenditure, this would not significantly alter the distributional pattern they reveal.

Incidence

Any study concerned with the distributional impact of public expenditure has to identify accurately who are the actual beneficiaries of that expenditure, that is, those on whom the expenditure is incident. Two problems arise here. First, there is the question of public goods, that is, commodities, of which the classic example is military defence, which are non-excludable and non-rival in consumption and hence whose use (or the benefits therefrom) cannot be allocated to any specific individual or group of individuals. Related to this problem, and of more relevance to the services discussed in the main text, is the question of externalities. An individual's use of a particular service may benefit (or cost) not only the individual himself or herself, but others as well, that is, it may generate an 'external' benefit (or cost). A classic example is the case of vaccination, where if I decide to be vaccinated against a particular disease under the National Health Service, then this not only reduces the chances of my getting the disease, but also reduces the chance of your catching it off me. Other examples include the reduction in congestion on roads due to public transport subsidies and the increase in the value of properties adjacent to a house recently refurbished with the aid of a housing improvement grant. If such externalities exist, then to assume that public expenditure in a particular service is incident only upon the direct users of that service, as is done in almost all the relevant studies, is incorrect.

The second problem concerns the possible shifting of the expenditure. An example of this discussed in the main text is the possible capitalisation of tax subsidies to owner-occupiers in house prices. That is, under certain conditions, the price of a house for owner-occupation will include the value of the tax subsidy, a situation which could imply that the principal beneficiary of the subsidy is not the existing owner, but one who owned the house when the subsidy was introduced. It was also noted in the relevant chapters that improvement grants and public transport subsidies may be capitalised in house prices in a similar manner.

But the problem is not confined to house prices. The introduction of any programme involving public expenditure will have a variety of different effects throughout the economy. Obviously, the price of any commodity directly subsidised by the programme will alter, but so will the prices of any goods and services that are complementary to, or substitute for, the subsidised commodity.

As a result all people who consume all these commodities (or who are associated in any way with their production) will be affected. The increase in public expenditure will be financed by a rise in taxation, cuts in other areas of public expenditure and/or an increase in government borrowing. Each of these will have effects on different people's incomes and living standards, which in turn will have effects on prices and incomes. A proper analysis of the distributional impact of the programme should therefore take account of all these ramifications, but, not surprisingly given the magnitude of the task, most of the studies concerned make no attempt to do so.

It is difficult to know what impact the failure of the studies discussed in the main text to deal with either externalities or with the shifting problem might have on their results concerning the impact of public expenditure on inequality. However, it is worth noting that, to have a serious effect on the conclusions of the book, it would be necessary for any externalities that exist to be distributed in favour of the lower social groups, and/or for there to be substantial shifting in favour of those groups. Since neither of these appears to be particularly plausible for the social services, it is likely that even if these problems were properly taken into account, the basic conclusions would remain intact.

Valuation

A common criticism of empirical work in the area is that the studies concerned usually measure the distribution of the public costs of the services concerned rather than the distribution of their private benefits. Thus the distributional impact of, for instance, public education is generally measured by the cost of the (publicly funded) educational inputs consumed, rather than by the value which the individuals concerned place on their education. Among other things, this has the rather bizarre consequence that an increase in productivity within a public service would, so long as everything else remained constant, lead to a decline in the recorded amounts of services received by each user.

A possible solution to this problem is to replace the estimates based on the distribution of costs by ones based on the distribution of consumer surplus. But this itself is not immune from difficulties. First, the measurable proxy for consumer surplus (the area under the Marshallian demand curve) is only an accurate indicator of the value an individual derives from consuming a service if the income elasticity of demand for the service is zero. Second, any comparison of consumer surpluses across individuals requires that the marginal utility of income to each individual is the same, a particularly implausible requirement when the comparison is being made across different income groups. Third, the data requirements are considerable; in particular, to construct the relevant demand curves, it is necessary to obtain individual money valuations of their use of the service concerned.

The third problem could be resolved if market valuations were available. However, since, for virtually all the services concerned, private markets are non-existent, very small or heavily distorted, it is not clear whence such valuations would come. Alternatively, questionnaires could be used; but these are unreliable, since respondents face no particular incentive to tell the truth (and indeed if they suspect the information they reveal may be used in some way detrimental to their interests – such as in assessing their tax burden – may have a positive incentive to lie). Preference-revelation mechanisms have recently been devised involving payments to or from individuals whereby individuals can maximise the payments they receive (or minimise the ones they make) if they reveal their preferences for a commodity correctly (see Varian, 1978, pp. 200–3, for a useful summary). But these have the rather implausible requirement that individuals' true preferences for the commodities concerned are independent of the size of the transfers involved; also, they have yet to be tried out on any significant scale.

Aaron and McGuire (1970) have shown that, for a public good, if households' utility functions are identical and additively separable between the public good and all other commodities then a household's money valuation of the public good will be inversely proportional to the marginal utility of its income (a result which, incidentally, is true under these assumptions not just for public goods, but also for any commodity that is consumed equally by households – a point not made by Aaron and McGuire). But apart from the inherent implausibility of the assumptions, this procedure does not solve the problem of the unavailability of data, for it is now necessary to obtain information concerning differences in households' marginal utilities of income.

It is possible that underlying the concerns for, particularly, equality of public expenditure and equality of use expressed by social reformers is a more fundamental concern for equality of benefits. Hence the failure of studies examined in this book adequately to measure benefits is *potentially* a problem for its conclusion that public expenditure has failed to fulfil the hopes of those reformers. However, it is only *actually* a problem if the distribution of benefits is significantly less pro-rich than the distribution of use, a situation that would arise, for instance, if the benefits (net of costs) derived from each unit of the service used by higher social groups was significantly less than the net benefits derived by lower groups. However, it is difficult to see why, for any of the services concerned, this should occur.

Comparison

A major aim of studies of distribution of public expenditure (and/ or taxation) is to investigate whether the policy or policies concerned have created greater equality. Usually, the indicator of equality chosen is some form of final income, for instance, the sum of private money income, cash receipts from the state, the value of any publicly subsidised services consumed, minus all taxes paid. But in trying to determine whether or not greater equality in final income has been achieved, the studies concerned encounter the problem discussed in Chapter 2 of choosing a distribution with which to compare the distribution of final income. Typically (as, for example, in the CSO studies) this is the distribution of 'original' income, that is, private money income before tax or any receipts from the state, whether in cash or in kind.

The use of the distribution of original income as the focus of comparison has been heavily criticised (see, for example, Prest, 1968, and Peacock, 1974). This is not because it is a hypothetical distribution, for, as Peacock says, 'much of economic analysis involves comparisons with hypothetical situations' (p. 153); rather, it is because it is a peculiarly unlikely one. Prest puts the point strongly: 'It is inconceivable that [the distribution of pre-tax income] would remain unchanged if all government revenue and expenditure were abolished. We must therefore firmly reject the idea that any such [comparisons] are possible' (p. 88). And, while not everyone would go as far as this, there is little doubt that the argument has considerable force.

However, in this specific form, it is not of great importance to the conclusions of this book. By and large original income is used only for the purpose of grouping individuals or households, a procedure not without its problems but not subject to this particular difficulty. The distributions that are generally used for comparative purposes are ones that seem more appropriate in the context of the general argument, viz., either actual distributions in the past or the hypothetical distributions that would exist if the policy concerned were discontinued and some other pursued, including, in particular, increases in the cash subsidies to the poor.

Overall, therefore, it seems that, although the studies discussed in the main text suffer to a greater or lesser extent from the general methodological problems discussed in this appendix, this is not likely to invalidate the conclusions drawn therefrom.

APPENDIX B

Additional Tables

Table B.1   *Public Expenditure by Programme, 1978–9*

£m. at 1979 Survey prices	*United Kingdom*
Agriculture, fisheries, food and forestry	897
Arts and libraries	399
Common services	1,022
Debt interest	2,941
Defence	7,502
Education	8,824
Environmental services	3,330
Government lending to nationalised industries	693
Health	7,688
Housing	5,256
Industry, energy, trade and employment	3,203
Law, order and protective services	2,329
Northern Ireland	2,233
Overseas aid and other overseas services	1,962
Personal social services	1,335
Research councils	293
Social security	18,266
Transport: road and rail	2,809
Transport: other	166
Other public services	958
Total public expenditure	72,106

Source: The Government's Expenditure Plans (1980, p. 16; Table 1.6, Table 2.6, pp. 58–9; Table 2.10, pp. 90–3; Table 2.11, pp. 100–1).

Table B.2   *Public Expenditure on the Social Services, 1978–9*

£m. at 1979 Survey prices	Great Britain
Education	
Current	
Under fives	182
Primary	1,833
Secondary	2,470
Other schools	526
Further education and teacher training	1,057
University	682
Student awards	638
Meals and milk	451
Miscellaneous services	451
Total current	8,290
Capital	
Under fives	14
Primary, secondary and other schools	348
Further education and teacher training	73
University	84
Miscellaneous services	15
Total capital	534
Total current and capital	8,824
Health	
Current	
Hospital and community health services	5,287
Family practitioner services:	
General medical services	451
General dental services	261
General ophthalmic services	60
Pharmaceutical services	879
Central health services	306
Total current	7,244
Capital	
Hospital and community health services	432
Family practitioner services	1
Central health services	11
Total capital	444
Total current and capital	7,688

Table B.2 (*contd.*)

£m. at 1979 Survey prices	Great Britain

Housing

Current
General subsidies — 1,872
Rent rebates and allowances — 556
Option mortgages — 170
Administration — 78

Total current — 2,676

Capital
Council housing — 1,853
Improvement grants — 119
Other grants and loans — 605

Total capital[a] — 2,579

Total current and capital[a] — 5,256

Personal Social Services

Current
Residential Care — 580
Day Care — 162
Community care — 287
Other local authority services — 233
Central government services — 12

Total current[a] — 1,273

Capital
Residential, day, community care and other local authority services — 61
Central government services — 1

Total capital — 62

Total current and capital — 1,335

Public transport

Current
British Rail passenger subsidies — 384
Other grants to British Rail — 154
Bus, underground and ferry services — 187
Concessionary fares — 119
Other — 21

Total current — 865

Table B.2 (*contd.*)

£m. at 1979 Survey prices	*Great Britain*
Capital	
Local public transport investment	240
New bus grant	28
Total capital	268
Total current and capital	1,133
Roads	
Current	764
Capital	725
Total current and capital	1,489
Transport administration	187

^a Totals do not add up in the source table.

Source: *The Government's Expenditure Plans* (1980, Table 2.6, pp. 58–9; Table 2.7, pp. 66–8; Table 2.10, pp. 90–1; Table 2.11, pp. 100–1; p. 107, Tables 2.11.7 and 2.11.8).

Table B.3 Public Expenditure on the Social Services by Income Group: CSO Estimates

All households

United Kingdom, 1978

Income group[a]	Expenditure per household (£ p.a.)					
	Health care	Education	School meals, milk and other welfare foods	Housing	Rail travel	All social services[b]
Top 20%	354	444	21	57	25	902
Next 20%	323	400	24	73	11	831
Middle 20%	320	348	26	103	7	804
Next 20%	309	216	22	118	5	670
Bottom 20%	306	156	22	205	2	691
Mean	322	313	23	111	10	780

[a] Original income.
[b] Includes food subsidies (= £1 p.a. for each group). Totals do not add up because of rounding.
Source: CSO (1980, Table 3, p. 116) and unpublished data provided by CSO.

Income and Occupational Classifications

This appendix gives details concerning the principal income and occupational classifications that are used in the main text.

Income

There are four conceptions of income that appear in the literature: original income, gross income, disposable income and final income. *Original income* is used to classify households in the annual studies of the effects of taxes and benefits produced by the Central Statistical Office (CSO) where it is defined as all income received from employment, occupational pensions and private investments (including rent, dividend payments, interest payments, etc.). Up to, and including the 1978 study, it also included income 'imputed' to owner-occupiers and those living in rent-free accommodation for the housing services they receive (for the rationale for considering these as income, see Chapter 5, p. 91); for some reason, imputed income for owner-occupiers has been omitted from the 1979 study (CSO, 1981, p. 118). It thus reflects income before any state intervention in the form of taxation, social security payments or the provision of public services. Care needs to be taken over its exact interpretation. In particular, it should not be interpreted as the income that the household concerned would have had if there had been no state intervention, since the household's decisions in those circumstances concerning its work and savings patterns would have been quite different – as would therefore its income.

Gross income refers to original income plus social security payments; it is used as a classificatory device primarily by non-government studies based directly on the Family Expenditure Survey. *Disposable income* is gross income minus direct taxes. *Final income* is disposable income minus indirect taxes plus the value of public services used (usually approximated by the cost of these services). Neither of these is generally used for grouping individuals or households; instead they (particularly final income) are used as indicators of greater or lesser equality between groups defined according to some other criterion.

Occupation

There are several different ways in which occupations have been classified in the studies reviewed in this book. The two principal ones are social class and socio-economic group, and these are discussed below; the others are outlined briefly in the chapters where they appear.

Social Class

Since 1911, the Registrar General has grouped occupations in the social classes. The occupations 'included in each of these categories have been selected so as to ensure that, so far as is possible, each category is homogeneous in relation to the basic criterion of the general standing within the community of the occupations concerned' (OPCS, 1970, p. x). There are five basic social classes (see Table C.1). For research purposes, the third (skilled) group is often split into manual and non-manual components. Table C.1 provides some basic information concerning the classes, including their descriptive definition, their proportions in the economically active and retired population and examples of the occupations included.

In the proportions listed in Table C.1 women have been allocated to social classes according to their own occupation. However, it should be noted that in the case of married women this is not the rule; they are usually allocated according to their husband's occupation. Children are generally allocated according to their father's occupation.

Socio-Economic Group

In the 1961 and 1971 Censuses occupations were classified not only into social classes, but into seventeen socio-economic groups

Table C.1   *Occupational Classification by Social Class*

Descriptive definition	*Registrar General's number*	*Proportion in population[a]*	*Examples*
Professional	I	4	Doctors, lawyers, architects, clergymen
Intermediate	II	18	Sales managers, teachers, nurses
Skilled non-manual	III(N)	21	Clerical workers, draughtsmen, shop assistants
Skilled manual	III(M)	28	Railway guards, bricklayers, miners (underground), electricians
Partly skilled	IV	21	Agricultural workers, barmen, bus conductors
Unskilled	V	8	Labourers, office cleaners, railway porters

[a] Population is all economically active or retired persons in Great Britian, 1971.
Sources: Figures from Reid (1977, p. 64, Table 3.1). Other information from OPCS (1970).

Table C.2   *Occupational Classification by Socio-Economic Group*

Descriptive definition	*Registrar General's SEG numbers*	*Proportion in population[a]*	*Examples*
Professionals, employers and managers	1, 2, 3, 4, 13	20	Doctors, lawyers, architects, clergymen, sales managers
Intermediate and junior non-manual	5, 6	21	Teachers, nurses, clerical workers, draughtsmen, shop assistants
Skilled manual	8, 9, 12, 14	36	Railway guards, foremen, bricklayers, miners (underground), electricians
Semi- and unskilled manual	7, 10, 11, 15	24	Agricultural workers, barmen, bus conductors, labourers, office cleaners, railway porters

[a] Population is all persons in General Household Survey sample in Great Britain, 1978.
Sources: Figures from OPCS (1980, p. 125, Table 7.15). Other information from OPCS (1970).

(SEGs). In official government surveys, such as the General Household Survey, these are often condensed into six categories; however, even some of these are too small for the distributional evidence reviewed in this book, and they have been further condensed into four basic SEGs. Table C.2 provides information concerning the four categories, again including their descriptive definitions, their proportions in the population and some examples of the kinds of occupation they include.

The following points should be noted. SEG categories 16 (members of the armed forces) and 17 (occupation inadequately described) are omitted. Men, single women, and married women whose husbands are not a member of the household are classified according to their own present or most recent occupation. Married women whose husbands are a member of the household are classified according to their husband's occupation. Children under 15 are classified by their father's occupation if the father is a member of the household, by their mother's if there is no father in the household, and by the head of the household if there is no parent. Adults who have never worked and who do not fit into any of the above categories are omitted.

Bibliography

Aaron, H. (1972), *Shelter and Subsidies: Who Benefits from Federal Housing Policies?* (Washington, D.C.: Brookings Institution).

Aaron, H. and McGuire, M. (1970), 'Public goods and income distribution', *Econometrica*, vol. 38, no. 6, pp. 907–20.

Abel-Smith, B. (1976), *Value for Money in Health Services* (London: Heinemann).

Abel-Smith, B. (1958), 'Whose welfare state?', in N. McKenzie (ed.), *Conviction*, (London: McGibbon, 1958), pp. 55–73.

Alderson, M. R. (1970), 'Social class and the health service', *Medical Officer*, vol. 124, pp. 51–9.

Allen, V. L. (1970), 'Theoretical issues in poverty research', *Journal of Social Issues*, vol. 26, no. 2, pp. 149–67.

Anderson, F. R., Kneese, A. V., Reed, P. D., Stevenson, R. B. and Taylor, S. (1977), *Environmental Improvement Through Economic Incentives* (Baltimore: Johns Hopkins University Press).

Atkinson, A. B. and Stiglitz, J. E. (1980), *Lectures on Public Economics* (New York: McGraw Hill).

Backett, M. (1977), 'Health services' in F. Williams (ed.), *Why the Poor Pay More* (London: National Consumer Council), pp. 93–129.

Barna, T. (1945), *Redistribution of Incomes Through Public Finance in 1937* (Oxford: Oxford University Press).

Baumol, W. J. and Bowen, W. G. (1966), *Performing Arts: the Economic Dilemma* (New York: Twentieth Century Fund).

Becker, G. (1975), 'Human capital and the personal distribution of income: an analytical approach'. Originally published as Woytinsky lecture, University of Michigan. Also published as Addendum to Ch. III of G. Becker, *Human Capital*, 2nd edn (New York: Columbia University Press).

Black, D. (1980), *Inequalities in Health*, report of a research working group chaired by Sir Douglas Black (London: Department of Health and Social Security).

Blaug, M., Dougherty, C. and Psacharopoulos, G. (1980), 'The distribution of schooling and the distribution of earnings: evidence from the British ROSLA of 1972', London School of Economics.

Bloch, P. B. (1974), *Equality of Distribution of Police Services: A Case Study of Washington D.C.* (Washington D.C.: Urban Institute).

Board of Inland Revenue (1979), *Inland Revenue Statistics 1979* (London: HMSO).

Boreham, A. and Semple, M. (1976), 'Future development of work in the government statistical service on the distribution and redistribution of household income', in A. B. Atkinson (ed.), *The Personal Distribution of Incomes* (London: George Allen & Unwin), pp. 269–312.

Bosanquet, N. (1980a), 'Health' in N. Bosanquet and P. Townsend (eds), *Labour and Equality* (London: Heinemann), pp. 205–25.

Bosanquet, N. (1980b), 'Labour and public expenditure: an overall view', in N. Bosanquet and P. Townsend (eds), *Labour and Equality* (London: Heinemann), pp. 24–43.

Boudon, R. (1974), *Education, Opportunity and Social Inequality* (London: Wiley).

Brown, G. W. and Harris, T. (1978), *Social Origins of Depression* (London: Tavistock).

Bruce, M. (1973) (ed.), *The Rise of the Welfare State* (London: Weidenfeld and Nicolson).

Buchan, I. and Richardson, I. (1973), *Time Study of Consultations in General Practice*, Scottish Health Service Studies, No. 27 (London: HMSO).

Carter, C. O. and Peel, J. (1976) (eds), *Equalities and Inequalities in Health* (London: Academic Press).

Cartter, A. M. (1955), *The Redistribution of Income in Postwar Britain* (New Haven: Yale University Press).

Cartwright, A. (1964), *Human Relations and Hospital Care*, Institute of Community Studies Series (London: Routledge and Kegan Paul).

Cartwright, A. and O'Brien, M. (1976), 'Social class variations in health care and in the nature of general practitioner consultations', in M. Stacey (ed.), *The Sociology of the National Health Service*, Sociological Review Monograph, no. 22 (Keele: Keele University Press), pp. 77–98.

Central Statistical Office (1975), *Social Trends* (London: HMSO).

Central Statistical Office (1980), 'The effects of taxes and benefits on household income, 1978' *Economic Trends*, no. 315 (January), pp. 99–135.

Central Statistical Office (1981), 'The effects of taxes and benefits on household income, 1979' *Economic Trends*, no. 327 (January), pp. 104–31.

Cochrane, A. L., St. Leger, A. S. and Moore, F. (1978), 'Health Service "input" and mortality "output" in developed countries', *Journal of Epidemiology and Community Health*, vol. 32, no. 3; pp. 200–5.

Collard, D. (1978), *Altruism and Economy* (Oxford: Martin Robertson).

Collins, E. and Klein, R. (1980), 'Equity and the NHS: self-reported morbidity, access and primary care', *British Medical Journal*, vol. 281, no. 6248, pp. 1111–15.

Cooper, A. J. and Cooper, M. H. (1972), *An International Price Comparison of Pharmaceuticals* (London: National Economic

Development Council).

Craig, F. W. S. (1975), *British General Election Manifestos, 1900–1974* (London: Macmillan).

Crosland, C. A. R. (1956), *The Future of Socialism* (London: Jonathan Cape).

Crosland, C. A. R. (1974), *Socialism Now* (London: Jonathan Cape).

Crouch, C. (1981), 'The place of public expenditure in socialist thought', in D. Lipsey and D. Leonard (eds), *The Socialist Agenda: Crosland's Legacy* (London: Jonathan Cape).

Culyer, A. J. (1976), *Need and the National Health Service* (London: Martin Robertson).

Culyer, A. J. (1980), *The Political Economy of Social Policy* (Oxford: Martin Robertson).

Davies, B. (1968), 'The cost-effectiveness of education spending' in *Social Services for All? Part Two*, Fabian Tract, no. 383 (London: Fabian Society).

Davies, B. (1978), *Universality, Selectivity and Effectiveness in Social Policy* (London: Heinemann).

Davis, K. (1977), 'A decade of policy developments in providing health care for low-income families', in R. Haveman (ed.) *A Decade of Federal Antipoverty Programs* (New York: Academic Press), pp. 197–231.

Davis, K. and Reynolds, R. (1975), 'Medicare and the utilisation of health care services by the elderly', *Journal of Human Resources*, vol. 10, no. 3, pp. 361–77.

de Lone, R. H. (1979), *Small Futures* (New York: Harcourt Brace Jovanovich).

Department of Education and Science (1967), *Children and Their Primary Schools*, Vol. 1, a report of the Central Advisory Council for Education (England), chaired by Lady Plowden (London: HMSO).

Department of Education and Science (1979), *Statistics of Education 1977, Vol. 5: Finance and Awards* (London: HMSO).

Department of Employment (1978), *Family Expenditure Survey, 1977* (London: HMSO).

Department of Employment (1979), *Family Expenditure Survey, 1978* (London: HMSO).

Department of Health and Social Security (1976), *Sharing Resources for Health in England*, report of the Resources Allocation Working Party (London: HMSO).

Department of the Environment (1979), *English House Conditions Survey, 1976, Part 2: Report of the Social Survey* (London: HMSO).

Department of the Environment (1980), *Housing and Construction Statistics 1969–1979* (London: HMSO).

Department of the Environment (1977), *Housing Policy, Technical Volume*, Part I (London: HMSO).

Department of the Environment (1976), *Transport Policy: A Consultation Document,* Vols 1 and 2 (London: HMSO).

Department of Transport (1979a), *National Travel Survey: 1975/6 Report* (London: HMSO).

Department of Transport (1979b), *Transport Statistics, Great Britain 1968–1978* (London: HMSO).

Earthrowl, B. and Stacey, M. (1977), 'Social class and children in hospital', *Social Science and Medicine,* vol. 11, no. 2, pp. 83–8.

Educational Reconstruction (1943), Cmd 6458 (London: HMSO).

Evetts, J. (1970), 'Equality of educational opportunity: the recent history of a concept', *British Journal of Sociology,* vol. 21, pp. 425–30.

Fair Deal For Housing (1971), Cmnd 4728 (London: HMSO).

Feldstein, M. (1975), 'Wealth neutrality and local choice in public education', *American Economic Review,* vol. 65, pp. 75–89.

Field, F., Meacher, M. and Pond, C. (1977), *To Him Who Hath* (Harmondsworth: Penguin).

Fields, G. (1975), 'Higher education and income distribution in a less-developed country', *Oxford Economic Papers,* vol. 27, no. 2, pp. 245–59.

Forster, D. P. (1979), 'The relationship between health needs, socio-environmental indices, general practitioner resources and utilisation', *Journal of Chronic Diseases,* vol. 32, no. 4, pp. 333–7.

Forster, D. P. (1976), 'Social class differences in sickness and general practitioner consultations', *Health Trends,* vol. 8, no. 2, pp. 29–32.

Friedman, L. S. and Wiseman, M. (1978), 'Understanding the equity consequences of school-finance reform', *Harvard Educational Review,* vol. 48, no. 2, pp. 193–226.

Friedman, M. and Friedman, R. (1980), *Free to Choose* (London: Secker and Warburg).

Fuchs, V. (1974), *Who Shall Live? Health, Economics and Social Choice* (New York: Basic Books).

Gardner, M. J., Crawford, M. D. and Morris, J. N. (1969), 'Patterns of mortality in middle and early old age in the county boroughs of England and Wales', *British Journal of Preventative and Social Medicine,* vol. 23, no. 2, pp. 133–40.

Gatherer, A., Parfit, J., Parter, E. and Vessey, M. (1979), *Is Health Education Effective?* Monograph No. 2 (London: Health Education Council).

Gillespie, W. (1965), 'Effect of public expenditures on the distribution of income', in R. A. Musgrave (ed.), *Essays in Fiscal Federalism* (Washington, D.C.: Brookings Institution).

Goldthorpe, J. H. (1980), *Social Mobility and Class Structure in Modern Britain* (Oxford: Oxford University Press).

Gough, I. (1979), *The Political Economy of the Welfare State* (London: Macmillan).

The Government's Expenditure Plans, 1980–81 to 1983–84 (1980), Cmnd 7841 (London: HMSO).

Greater London Council (1974), *Supplementary Licensing* (London: Greater London Council).

Grey, A. (1975), *Urban Fares Policy* (Farnborough: Saxon House).

Grey, A., Hepworth, N. and Odling-Smee, J. (1978), *Housing Rents, Costs and Subsidies* (London: Chartered Institute of Public Finance and Accountancy).

Halsey, A. H. (1972) (ed.), *Educational Priority, Vol. 1: E.P.A. Problems and Policies* (London: HMSO).

Halsey, A. H., Heath, A. F. and Ridge, J. M. (1980), *Origins and Destinations* (Oxford: Oxford University Press, 1980).

Hansen, W. and Weisbrod, B. (1969), 'The distribution of the costs and direct benefits of public higher education: the case of California', *Journal of Human Resources*, vol. 4, no. 2, pp. 176–91.

Hansen, W. and Weisbrod, B. (1978), 'The distribution of subsidies to students in California public higher education: reply', *Journal of Human Resources*, vol. 13, no. 1, pp. 137–9.

Harbury, C. D. and Hitchens, D. M. W. N. (1979), *Inheritance and Wealth Inequality in Britain* (London: George Allen & Unwin).

Harrison, A. (1979), *The Distribution of Wealth in Ten Countries*, Royal Commission on the Distribution of Income and Wealth, Background Paper no. 7 (London: HMSO).

Higher Education (1963), Report of the Committee on Higher Education, chaired by Lord Robbins. Cmnd 2154. (London: HMSO, 1963).

Housing Policy (1977), Cmnd 6851 (London: HMSO).

Hughes, G. A. (1979), 'Housing Income and Subsidies', *Fiscal Studies*, vol. 1, no. 1, pp. 20–38.

Illich, I. (1976), *Limits to Medicine* (London: Marion Boyars).

Jencks, C. (1972), *Inequality* (New York: Basic Books).

Jencks, C. (1979), *Who Gets Ahead?* (New York: Basic Books).

Joseph, K. and Sumption, J. (1979), *Equality* (London: John Murray).

Judy, R. (1970), 'The income distributive effects of aid to higher education', in L. H. Officer and L. B. Smith (eds), *Canadian Economic Problems and Policies* (New York: McGraw-Hill), pp. 302–17.

Kay, J. and King, M. A. (1978), *The British Tax System* (Oxford: Oxford University Press).

Keynes, J. M. (1936), *The General Theory of Employment, Interest and Money* (London: Macmillan).

King, M. A. and Atkinson, A. B. (1980), 'Housing policy, taxation and reform' *Midland Bank Review* (Spring), pp. 7–15.

Lansley, S. (1979), *Housing and Public Policy* (London: Croom Helm).

Leech, D. and Cowling, K. (1978), 'Health, income and social class', paper presented at the December 1978 meeting of the SSRC Health Economists' Study Group.

Le Grand, J. (1978), 'The distribution of public expenditure: the case of health care', *Economica*, vol. 45, pp. 125–42.

Le Grand, J. (1980), 'The distribution of public expenditure on education', London School of Economics. Forthcoming in *Economica*.

Le Grand, J. (1981), 'Equity as an economic objective', London School of Economics.

Le Grand, J. (1975), 'Public price discrimination and aid to low income groups', *Economica*, vol. 42, pp. 32–42.

Le Grand, J. (1978), 'Who benefits from public expenditure?' *New Society*, vol. 45, no. 833, pp. 614–16.

Le Grand, J. and Robinson, R. V. F. (1976), *The Economics of Social Problems* (London: Macmillan).

Lewis, O. (1966), *La Vida* (New York: Random House).

Lineberry, R. (1975), 'Equality, public policy and public services: the underclass hypothesis and the limits to equality', *Policy and Politics*, vol. 4, no. 2, pp. 67–84.

Lineberry, R. (1977), *Equality and Urban Policy* (Beverly Hills: Sage).

Lister, R. (1974), *Take-up of Means Tested Benefits* (London: Child Poverty Action Group).

McGuire, J. (1976), 'The distribution of costs and direct benefits of public education: the case of California', *Journal of Human Resources*, vol. 11, no. 3, pp. 343–53.

McGuire, J. (1978), 'Rejoinder', *Journal of Human Resources*, vol. 13, no. 1, pp. 139–41.

McKeown, T. (1976), *The Role of Medicine* (London: Nuffield Provincial Hospitals Trust).

Marshall, T. H. (1963), 'Citizenship and social class', in *Sociology at the Crossroads* (London: Heinemann), pp. 67–127.

Marshall, T. H. (1970), *Social Policy*, 3rd edn (London: Hutchinson).

Martini, C. J. M., Allan, G. B. J., Davison, J. and Backett, E. M. (1977), 'Health indices that are sensitive to medical care variation', *International Journal of Health Services*, vol. 7, no. 2, pp. 293–309.

Meacher, M. (1972), *Rate Rebates* (London: Child Poverty Action Group).

Meade, J. (1978), *The Structure and Reform of Direct Taxation*, report of a committee chaired by Professor J. E. Meade (London: Institute for Fiscal Studies).

Meerman, J. (1979), *Public Expenditure in Malaysia: Who Benefits and Why* (Oxford: Oxford University Press).

Merrett, A. J. and Monk, D. A. G. (1966), 'The structure of UK taxation, 1962–3', *Bulletin of the Oxford University Institute of Economics and Statistics*, vol. 28, no. 3, pp. 145–62.

Miller, S. M., Riessman, F. and Seagull, A. A. (1965), 'Poverty and self-indulgence: a critique of the non-deferred gratification pattern' in L.

A. Ferman, J. L. Kornbluth and A. Harber (eds), *Poverty in America* (Ann Arbor: University of Michigan).

Ministry of Education (1963), *Half Our Future*, a report of the Central Advisory Council for Education (England), chaired by John Newsom (London: HMSO).

Ministry of Transport (1964), *Road Pricing: The Economic and Technical Possibilities*, report of a panel chaired by R. Smeed (London: HMSO).

Ministry of Transport (1968), *Road Track Costs* (London: HMSO).

Morris, J. N. (1979), 'Social inequalities undiminished', *The Lancet*, no. 8107 (January 13), pp. 87–90.

Musgrave, R., Case, K. and Leonard, H. (1974), 'The distribution of fiscal burdens and benefits', *Public Finance Quarterly*, vol. 2, no. 3, pp. 259–311.

National Consumer Council (1976), *Means Tested Benefits* (London: National Consumer Council).

A National Health Service (1944), Cmd 6502, (London: HMSO).

Neave, G. (1976), *Patterns of Equality* (Windsor: NFER Publ. Co.).

Nicholson, J. L. (1964), 'Redistribution of income in the United Kingdom in 1959, 1957 and 1953', in International Association for Research in Income and Wealth, *Income and Wealth*, Series X (London: Bowes and Bowes).

Nicholson, J. L. and Britton, A. J. C. (1976), 'The redistribution of income', in A. B. Atkinson (ed.), *The Personal Distribution of Incomes*, (London: George Allen & Unwin), pp. 317–34.

Noyce, J., Snaith, A. and Trickey, A. J. (1974), 'Regional variations in the allocation of financial resources to the community health services', *The Lancet*, no. 7857 (March 30), pp. 554–7.

Office of Health Economics (1979), *Compendium of Health Statistics*, 3rd edn (London: Office of Health Economics).

Office of Population Censuses and Surveys (1970), *Classification of Occupations, 1970* (London: HMSO).

Office of Population Censuses and Surveys (1975), *The General Household Survey, 1972* (London: HMSO).

Office of Population Censuses and Surveys (1976), *The General Household Survey, 1973* (London: HMSO).

Office of Population Censuses and Surveys (1978), *The General Household Survey, 1976* (London: HMSO).

Office of Population Censuses and Surveys (1979), *The General Household Survey, 1977* (London: HMSO).

Office of Population Censuses and Surveys (1980), *The General Household Survey, 1978* (London: HMSO).

O'Higgins, M. (1980), 'The distributive effects of public expenditure and taxation: an agnostic view of the CSO analyses', in C. Sandford, C. Pond and R. Walker (eds), *Taxation and Social Policy* (London:

Heinemann), pp. 15–46.

Owen, D. (1981), *Face the Future* (London: Jonathan Cape).

Owen, D. (1976), *In Sickness and In Health* (London: Quartet).

Papanicolalaou, J. and Psacharopoulos, G. (1979), 'Socioeconomic background, schooling and monetary rewards in the United Kingdom', *Economica*, vol. 46, pp. 435–9.

Peacock, A. T. (1974), 'The treatment of government expenditure in studies of income redistribution' in W. L. Smith and J. M. Culbertson (eds), *Public Finance and Stabilization Policy* (Amsterdam: North-Holland), pp. 151–67.

Peacock, A. T. and Browning, P. (1956), 'The social services in Great Britain and the redistribution of income', in A. Peacock (ed.), *Income Redistribution and Social Policy* (London: Jonathan Cape), pp. 139–77.

Peacock, A. T. and Shannon, R. (1968), 'The welfare state and the redistribution of income', *Westminster Bank Review* (August), pp. 30–46.

Peacock, A. T. and Wiseman, J. (1961), *The Growth of Public Expenditure in the United Kingdom* (Princeton, N.J.: Princeton University Press).

Pechman, J. (1970), 'The distributional effects of public higher education in California', *Journal of Human Resources*, vol. 5, no. 3, pp. 361–70.

Peretz, J. (1975), 'Beneficiaries of public expenditure: an analysis for 1971/2', Central Statistical Office.

Piachaud, D. (1975), 'The economics of educational opportunity', *Higher Education*, vol. 4, pp. 201–12.

Piachaud, D. (1979), 'Inequality and social policy', *New Society*, vol. 47, no. 855, pp. 670–2.

Prest, A. R. (1968), 'The budget and interpersonal distribution', *Public Finance*, vol. 23, nos 1/2, pp. 80–98.

Pryke, R. and Dodgson, J. (1975), *The Rail Problem* (London: Martin Robertson).

Psacharopoulos, G. (1981), 'Education and society: old myths versus new facts', in Lord Roll (ed.), *The Mixed Economy* (London: Macmillan).

Psacharopoulos, G. (1977a), 'Family background, education and achievement: a path model of earnings determinants in the UK and some alternatives', *British Journal of Sociology*, vol. 28, no. 3, pp. 321–35.

Psacharopoulos, G. (1977b), 'The perverse effects of public subsidization of education', *Comparative Education Review*, vol. 21, no. 1, pp. 69–90.

Reid, I. (1977), *Social Class Differences in Britain: A Sourcebook* (London: Open Books).

Reynolds, M. and Smolensky, E. (1977), *Public Expenditure, Taxes and the Distribution of Income: The U.S., 1950, 1961, 1970* (New York: Academic Press).

Robinson, R. V. F. (1979), *Housing Economics and Public Policy* (London: Macmillan).

Robinson, R. V. F. (1980), 'Housing tax-expenditures, subsidies and the distribution of income', University of Sussex. Forthcoming in *Manchester School*.

Robson, W. A. (1976), *Welfare State and Welfare Society* (London: George Allen & Unwin).

Rogers, R. (1980), 'The myth of the "independent" schools', *New Statesman*, vol. 99, no. 2546 (January 4), pp. 10–12.

Rosenthal, L. (1977), 'The regional and income distribution of the council house subsidy in the United Kingdom', *Manchester School*, vol. 45, no. 2, pp. 127–40.

Routh, G. (1980), *Occupation and Pay in Great Britain, 1906–79* (London: Macmillan).

Royal Commission on the Distribution of Income and Wealth (1980), *An A to Z of Income and Wealth* (London: HMSO).

Royal Commission on the Distribution of Income and Wealth (1979), *Report No. 8*, Cmnd 7679 (London: HMSO).

Royal Commission on the National Health Service (1979), *Report*, Cmnd 7615 (London: HMSO).

Ruggles, P. (1979), *The Allocation of Taxes and Benefits to Households in the United States*, unpublished PhD dissertation, Harvard.

Rutter, M., Maugham, B., Mortimer, P. and Ouston, J. (1979), *Fifteen Thousand Hours* (London: Open Books).

Saunders, C. and Marsden, D. (1979), *A Six-Country Comparison of the Distribution of Industrial Earnings in the 1970s*, Royal Commission on the Distribution of Income and Wealth, Background Paper No. 8 (London: HMSO).

Schneider, L. S. and Lysgaard, S. (1953), 'The deferred gratification pattern: a preliminary study', *American Sociological Review*, vol. 18, no. 2, pp. 142–9.

Select Committee on Nationalised Industries (1977), *First Report*, House of Commons 1976–77, 305-I (London: HMSO).

Selowsky, M. (1979), *Who Benefits from Government Expenditure: A Case Study of Colombia* (Oxford: Oxford University Press).

Sleeman, J. F. (1973), *The Welfare State* (London: George Allen & Unwin).

Social Insurance and Allied Services (1942), Report by Sir William Beveridge, Cmd 6404 (London: HMSO).

Stark, T. (1977), *The Distribution of Income in Ten Countries*, Royal Commission on the Distribution of Income and Wealth, Background Paper No. 4 (London: HMSO).

Stigler, G. J. (1970), 'Director's law of public income redistribution',

Journal of Law and Economics, vol. 13, no. 1, pp. 1–10.

Sugarman, B. (1970), 'Social class and family life', in M. Craft (ed.), *Family, Class and Education*, (London: Longman), pp. 241–54.

Szakolczai, G. (1980), 'Limits to redistribution: the Hungarian experience', in D. Collard, R. Lecomber and M. Slater (eds), *Income Distribution: the Limits to Redistribution* (Bristol: John Wright), pp. 206–35.

Tawney, R. H. (1964), *Equality*, first published in 1931, references are to 1964 edition (London: George Allen & Unwin).

Throsby, C. D. and Withers, G. A. (1979), *Economics of the Performing Arts* (London: Edward Arnold).

Titmuss, R. (1968), *Commitment to Welfare* (London: George Allen & Unwin).

Titmuss, R. (1970), *The Gift Relationship* (London: George Allen & Unwin).

Tobin, J. (1970), 'On limiting the domain of inequality', *Journal of Law and Economics*, vol. 13, no. 2, pp. 263–77.

Townsend, P. (1974), 'Inequality and the health service', *The Lancet*, no. 7868 (June 15), pp. 1179–90.

Townsend, P. (1979), *Poverty in the United Kingdom* (Harmondsworth: Penguin).

Townsend, P. (1975), *Sociology and Social Policy* (London: Allen Lane).

Transport Policy (1977), Cmnd 6836 (London: HMSO).

Varian, H. (1978), *Micro-economic Analysis* (New York: W. W. Norton).

Weaver, F. (1950), 'Taxation and redistribution in the United Kingdom', *Review of Economics and Statistics*, vol. 32, no. 3, pp. 201–13.

Webb, A. (1980), 'The personal social services' in N. Bosanquet and P. Townsend (eds), *Labour and Equality* (London: Heinemann), pp. 279–95.

Webb, A. and Sieve, J. E. B. (1971), *Income Redistribution and the Welfare State*, Occasional Papers in Social Administration, No. 41 (London: Bell).

Weicher, J. (1971), 'The allocation of police protection by income class', *Urban Studies*, vol. 8, no. 3, pp. 207–20.

Whitehead, C. (1980), 'Fiscal aspects of Housing' in C. Sandford, C. Pond and R. Walker (eds), *Taxation and Social Policy* (London: Heinemann), pp. 84–114.

Whitehead, C. (1977), 'Where have all the dwellings gone?', *Centre for Environmental Studies Review*, vol. 1, no. 1, pp. 45–53.

Wilensky, H. (1975), *The Welfare State and Equality* (Berkeley: University of California Press).

Wilkinson, R. (1976a), 'Dear David Ennals ...', *New Society*, vol. 38, no. 741, pp. 567–8.

Wilkinson, R. (1976b), *Socioeconomic Factors in Mortality Differentials*,

M. Med. Sci. Thesis, University of Nottingham.

Willis, J. R. M. and Hardwick, P. J. W. (1978), *Tax Expenditures in the United Kingdom* (London: Institute of Fiscal Studies).

Windham, D. M. (1970), *Education, Equality and Income Redistribution* (Lexington, Mass.: D. C. Heath).

Witt, S. F. and Newbould, G. D. (1976), 'The impact of food subsidies', *National Westminster Bank Quarterly Review* (August), pp. 29–36.

Yates, J. (1979), 'The distributional impact of subsidies arising from the non-taxation of imputed rent in Australia: 1966–1968', University of Leicester, Public Sector Economics Research Centre Discussion Paper 79/04.

Index

For Product Safety Concerns and Information please contact our EU
representative GPSR@taylorandfrancis.com
Taylor & Francis Verlag GmbH, Kaufingerstraße 24, 80331 München, Germany